Good-bye Heathcliff

Recent Titles in
Contributions in Women's Studies

GOOD-BYE HEATHCLIFF

Changing Heroes, Heroines,
Roles, and Values in
Women's Category Romances

MARIAM DARCE FRENIER

CONTRIBUTIONS IN WOMEN'S STUDIES, NUMBER 94

GREENWOOD PRESS

New York · Westport, Connecticut · London

823.085
Frenier

Library of Congress Cataloging-in-Publication Data

Frenier, Mariam Darce, 1936–
  Good-bye Heathcliff : changing heroes, heroines, roles, and values
in women's category romances / Mariam Darce Frenier.
      p. cm.—(Contributions in women's studies, ISSN 0147-104X ;
no. 94)
  Bibliography: p.
  Includes index.
  ISBN 0-313-26088-5 (lib. bdg. : alk. paper)
  1. Love stories, English—Women authors—History and criticism.
2. English fiction—20th century—History and criticism. 3. Women
and literature—Great Britain—History—20th century. 4. Love
stories, American—Women authors—History and criticism.
5. American fiction—20th century—History and criticism. 6. Women
and literature—United States—History—20th century. 7. Women—
Books and reading—History—20th century. 8. Popular literature—
History and criticism. 9. Heroes in literature. 10. Heroines in
literature. 11. Sex role in literature. 12. Social values in
literature. I. Title. II. Series.
PR888.L69F74   1988
823'.085'099287—dc19   87-31786

British Library Cataloguing in Publication Data is available.

Library of Congress Catalog Card Number: 87-31786
ISBN: 0-313-26088-5
ISSN: 0147-104X

First published in 1988

Greenwood Press, Inc.
88 Post Road West, Westport, Connecticut 06881

Printed in the United States of America

The paper used in this book complies with the
Permanent Paper Standard issued by the National
Information Standards Organization (Z39.48-1984).

10 9 8 7 6 5 4 3 2 1

to Melanie Kaleck,
without her this would have been impossible

Contents

Acknowledgments

I would like to thank Harold Hinds who has been instrumental to the process of my development as a student of popular culture. He not only read parts of this manuscript, he shared his many theoretical insights. Finally, he gave much needed and welcomed moral support. I would also like to thank Emily Toth for her helpful theoretical and editorial comments on what became a part of this manuscript.

I also owe thanks to the librarians of the Rodney A. Briggs Library at the University of Minnesota Morris—especially May Jesseph and Barb McGinnis—and of the Morris Municipal Library—especially Rita Mulcahy. In addition, I must especially thank the UMM Division of Social Science secretaries, Bonnie Storck and Char Syverson.

Direct editorial help came from Charlie Fowler and my son Will Adams. Thanks to them for all their help.

Last but never least, I wish to thank those of my colleagues, students, and friends—especially my bridge companions—who loyally stood behind me, even cheered me on, while I researched this "romance fluff."

Good-bye
Heathcliff

1

Introduction

When I began this study in the late 1970s, I could not understand why so many American women opposed the Equal Rights Amendment.* After all, Betty Friedan's *The Feminine Mystique*, a study of the cause of malaise among white middle-class women was "old hat" (Friedan, *The Feminine Mystique*, 1963). Over 2,300,000 copies of Marilyn French's *The Women's Room* were selling. Divorce rates had risen higher than ever before in American history, inflation had driven more married women to work outside the home, and battered wives were making the news. Women's status was discussed everywhere in the popular media—newspapers, magazines, television, radio—and usually that status was found wanting. How could women, bombarded with all this, oppose the E.R.A.?

I studied the opponents of the E.R.A. to see if they differed in any important ways from other American women. I found only two major differences. Opponents insist that men and women are

---

*The Equal Rights Amendment as passed by the United States Congress in 1972 and as reintroduced in May 1983:

Section 1. Equality of rights under the law shall not be denied or abridged by the United States or by any state on account of sex.

Section 2. The Congress shall have the power to enforce, by appropriate legislation, the provision of this article.

Section 3. This amendment shall take effect two years after the date of ratification.

inherently different; they believe that 1950s white American gender stereotypes are "traditional" and properly differentiate the sexes.
Second, they are more likely to be fundamentalist and evangelical
Protestants than the American population as a whole. Fundamentalist Protestants usually agree that the 1950s white woman and
man exemplified America's best. Concentrating on this second observation, I read and watched Jerry Falwell, Pat Robertson, and
other electric media fundamentalists. I soon realized that these
missionaires were not doing much in the way of "selling" the 1950s
womanly ideal, in that they didn't offer much in the way of rewards to women for living up to it. (The image of Tammy Faye
Bakker, dominating religious news in 1987, only confused these
issues.) Where and how, I pondered, was that role sold and re-
warded? Especially, where and how was it sold to adult American
women? The obvious answer—American mass media.

First, it is possible that today popular media functions as religion in the United States. Among the many students of popular
culture who ponder this question is George H. Lewis, who said
that "contemporary culture (especially popular culture) may well
be playing the part religion once did" (Lewis, 1982: 86). Further,
I reasoned that the media might present a mythological 1950s
woman in such a way that some women can believe that living as
she did obviates any need for equal rights. I assumed that women
lacking equal rights must be presented as having achieved rewards
more valuable than the attainment of equal rights.

These assumptions were informed by having myself been a 1950s
woman who attempted to live up to that era's white, middle-class
stereotype of good wife and mother. In the process, even as I was—
and behaved like—a battered wife, I knew a kind of "reverse ben-
efit," the power of the victim wife-mother, that has been ignored
in most feminist studies. Hence, my ironic concession that if patriarchy had remained "benevolent," I would probably have never
revolted against it. Looking back from the 1980s, I see that patriarchy was never truly benevolent, and that it hurts men as well
as women. Nevertheless, I remain fascinated by women's concept
of their own power or powerlessness, whether they identify themselves as traditional, modern, non-white, or use other standards.

Two more relevant insights occurred to me as I fought for re-
lease from a patriarchal marriage that had turned nasty. As indus-

trializing American society accelerated reliance on the individual instead of the community or family as its social unit, it fostered a nineteenth-century model of romantic love. This ideal tied an individual woman to an individual man regardless of family or community disapproval or interference. By the 1950s, idealistically, romantic love had evolved into an obsession with the loved one. Therefore, if a 1950s wife could be assured that her husband was obsessed by her, as she was encouraged by popular culture to be obsessed by and addicted to him, she had great power and a vested interest in the status quo.

The second insight occurred as I read and listened to statements made by women opposed to extensions of women's rights. Like their anti-suffrage predecessors, they inveighed against feminists not only because feminists asked for change but also because they represented new concepts of women's power. I asked, do feminists cause fear because we seem more powerful than traditional women, less powerful, or both?

Obsessive love and overt anti-feminism were major components of radio, movies, and popular novels in the 1950s. As television began to dominate all other popular media, it copied these established characteristics of romance. Television in the 1970s and 1980s has become the most important popular medium in the United States and one of the chief purveyors of ideas relating to women's "proper" role and exercise of power. However, only three corporations have major control over television programming (although the introduction of alternate cable channels is undermining that control). Since I wanted to look at a medium that was more consumer selected, I chose to study women's romances instead of television.

By 1982, an estimated 38 million adult American women readers (Collins, 1983: 60)—a number amounting to "one-third of the total adult female population" of the United States ("For Love," 1983:1C)—annually spent $300 million on romance fiction. In addition, as women activists opposed extensions of women's rights, the popularity of romances boomed after 1972.

Studying romances turned out to be a profitable way to grapple with several broad questions about "traditional" women. First of all, contradicting my first assumption, studies find that romance readers are not anti-feminists; for example, Carol Thurston found that 73 percent of them were pro-choice on reproductive rights, although only 58 percent supported the E.R.A. in 1987 (Thurston, Feb. 1987: 21). Second, while romances portray heroines in the changing context of the times, they continue to offer rewards to "unliberated" American women. However, those rewards changed from 1970 through 1987. I therefore asked how, in her relationship with the hero, did the power of the romance heroine change? And do the changed rewards tell us anything about white American women's fear or acceptance of feminism and feminists?

2

The Romance Industry

By 1983, American newspapers, television, *Time*, *Psychology Today*, and even *Forbes* noticed the romantic fiction phenomenon. Romances had become big business.

Basically, romance fiction comes in two forms: mass-market paperbacks and category romances. The mass-market paperbacks are, relative to the latter, formula-free and more expensive. The category romances are formulaic, written using publisher's guidelines, and sold under a brand name. Both types of romances sell at newsstands, variety stores, and supermarkets, as well as in bookstores. In addition, by 1983, romances had invaded the world of trade paperbacks. These soft-cover books are usually sold only in bookstores and cost more than mass-market paperbacks. Mid-1987 mass-market paperbacks ordinarily cost $3.95 or $4.95 and romance trade paperbacks cost from $3.95 to $9.95. (Hardback romances like those of the best-selling romance author of 1987 Danielle Steel, who never published as a category writer, sold for $18.95 and $19.95.)

By 1984, publishers like Avon, Dell, and Bantam depended on romances for a large share of their profit. Other money makers were ordinary mass-market authors who could earn $30,000 from a single volume (Reed, 1981: 101). Continuing into the 1980s, there were authors like Steel, Janet Dailey, Judith Krantz, and Barbara Cartland who were "cottage industries" earning huge figures. For example, in 1982 Dailey received a $2 million cash advance to write 28 books for Silhouette Books with royalties "well over 15 percent," according to her husband (Rudolph, 1982: 51). A second business tier was formed by newsletters rating romances and bookstores devoting their inventories to them. In addition, large sums were spent on television and magazine advertisements of romance fiction.

In the early 1980s, romance paperback annual sales totaled at least $300 million (Thurston, 1983: 14). Romances constituted over 30 percent of all mass-market paperback sales (Jennings, 1984: 52) and 40 percent of all paperback sales ("For Love," 1983: 1C). According to an article in *Forbes*, 1982 profits could "run 10 percent pretax" (Rudolph, 1982: 50). Comparing 1982 with 1981, the sale of all romances increased 46 percent (Maryles, 1983: 54). Given the surfeit of choices now available to them, readers' loyalty to category romances faded and they began to choose their books by authors (Jennings, 1984: 53).

By fall 1983, 150 new romances were coming off the presses during the average month ("For Love," 1983: 1C), and eight publishers were pumping out category romances. Harlequin Enterprises Limited, the forerunner, still stood at the top of its field. Its profits had soared from $7.7 million in 1970 (Wagner, 1976: 97) to $145 million in 1982, even though its market share dropped from 80 percent in 1979 to 58 percent (Collins, 1983: 66). These figures are not corrected for inflation.

Harlequin Enterprises Limited's slip in the market share was a result of "Romance Wars" begun in 1980. The first entrant to challenge Harlequin was Simon & Schuster's Silhouette line. Silhouette Books set out to determine what American women "really wanted to read," according to Andrew Ettinger, Los Angeles literary agent and publications consultant (Jennings, 1984: 50). P. J. Fennel, hired away from Harlequin by Simon & Schuster, instituted "consumer focus groups" in order to learn exactly what American readers desired (51).

By 1982, Silhouette Books had become Harlequin's nearest rival and claimed an annual sale of $35 million and a 20 percent share of the market for 1982. Other romance publishers entered the fray: Dell, Jove, Bantam, Avon, Ballantine, and New American Library. American drugstores and supermarkets were inundated with romances. Rack space devoted to category romances alone jumped 50 percent from 1980 to 1981 (Rudolph, 1983: 50). At B. Dalton, the largest chain of bookstores, romances accounted for 30 percent of mass-market paperbacks in stock by April 1981 (Reed, 1981: 101), and this did not take into account the category romances often placed in "dump displays" (displays of specific category lines) and special book racks. In 1982, B. Dalton's sales of series romances increased approximately 98 percent over 1981 (Maryles, 1983: 54).

Not only was the quantity of romances exploding, but between 1980 and 1983 a revolution occurred within the romance world. This was officially acknowledged in 1981 when Dell introduced Candlelight Ecstasy, the first line of romances "to meet the readers' expressed desire for sexier, spicier books. . . . It inspired strong brand loyalty in readers." In 1983, Candlelight Ecstasy was "the only romance line guaranteed to sell out in many bookstores on the same day the shipment is received" (Collins, 1983: 60, 65–66). These new romances were to be more "realistic." For example, Anne Gisonny, executive editor of Candlelight Ecstasy, explained: "Always assigning your male character the dominant position in a relationship, and always placing your heroine in a passive victimized role is fallacious and totally unrealistic" (Falk, 1983: 159). Thus gender role changes joined enhanced depictions of sensuality.

The revolution was also advanced by six new series of category romances introduced in 1983. Harlequin Enterprises Limited— adding to its Romance, Presents, and Superromance lines—launched Harlequin American Romances in April 1983. Unlike the Romance and Presents series which came out with six titles per month, the Harlequin American Romances came out four per month. Harlequin Enterprises Limited spent $5 million advertising and promoting this new line. Seventy-five percent of this money went to network television advertising, the rest for trade and consumer print ads (Maryles, 1983: 53–54). Other new lines were: Rapture Romances, introduced by New American Library in January; Finding Mr. Right, by Avon in February; Loveswept (an imitation of Second Chance at Love—in which heroines, often widowed or divorced, were granted second chances), by Bantam in April; Intimate Moments, by Silhouette Books in May; and in fall 1983, Berkly/Jove introduced To Have and To Hold, a series concerned with married couples (Maryles, 1983: 54–58).

In addition to published books, there were spin-off products. Newsletters arose from readers' desire for tips on which authors and titles to buy. The first newsletter editor—dubbed a "Romance Maven" by *Publishers Weekly*—was Kathryn Falk, who edited *Romantic Times*. Other newsletters were *Boy Meets Girl*, edited by Vivian Lee Jennings; *Affaire de Coeur*, published by Barbara Keenan; *Heartline*, edited by Terri Busch; and *Barbara Critiques*, edited by Barbara Wren.

Teen romances began in 1979, with Scholastic Books introducing its Wildfire Series, followed in 1980 by its Wishing Star. In February 1981, Dell started its Young Love line, and in September of that year Bantam issued Sweet Dreams. In October, Simon & Schuster came out with the First Love line of Silhouette Books. In February 1982, Grosset & Dunlop began Caprice, and in October Dutton launched Heavenly Romances (Kellog, 1983: 158). Teen romance heroines are about 15 or 16 and their heroes are slightly older. These romances contain no sexuality.

Fueling all this, as noted above, the number of romance readers was growing. Market analysts believed they knew these readers. One, Richard Flaxman, decided that they were conservative. He found that the romance reader "believes in traditional values and would be more comfortable in the 1950s than she is in the 80s. Her politics and her morality are conservative" (Falk, 1983: 114). Unfortunately for Flaxman, his analysis proved to be incorrect.

Market analysts, non-readers of romances, and, to their sorrow, even publishers of category romances dismissed women readers as mere ciphers in 1983. However, according to Carol Thurston's 1983 survey of American readers, half of the market had some college education and 40 percent were employed full time and watched less television than average Americans, preferring news and movies to soap operas. Their average family income was as high as $30,000 (Thurston, 1983: 14). Another income estimate was $22,000 for a family of four. Researchers found the ages of readers to be 18 to 60, and the most avid readers were aged 26 to 45. Readers were more likely to live in rural and suburban areas than in large cities (Campion, 1983: 99).

In 1984, figures on general readership showed the importance of prospective romance readers to the publishing market. The average reader of all books was a white woman under 50, college educated, single, affluent, and white-collar. Heavy readers spent 21.3 hours per week reading, bought 47 percent of the books they read, and read 24 books every 6 months (Reuter, 1984: 16).

What about the population of American romance readers? Thurston found that 20 percent read at least one romance a day, and that 40 percent read one every two days (Thurston, 1983: 14; see also Thurston, Feb. 1987: 20–22). Leonard Wood's figures indicate that in 1983 romances constituted the largest category of fiction books purchased by American women (26 percent), and that historical novels formed the second largest category (23 percent). Since most historical novels are romances, the combined percentage, 49 percent, illustrates the importance of romances to American publishers in 1983 (Wood, 1983: 30).

Attempting to keep up, publishers' print runs were extraordinary. Silhouette Books began in 1980 with 200,000 per title and by June of that year had increased its print run to 240,000. Advertising money was lavish; Silhouette spent $3 million for television advertising in 1980. At the peak of the romance battle, 1983, Harlequin Enterprises Limited and Silhouette Books were spending $20 million per year on total consumer advertising (Jennings, 1984: 51). By early 1983, the major bookstore chains, first Waldenbooks and then B. Dalton, began to operate romance book clubs. Using this format, readers could buy six romances and get one free.

With increased choice, readers were picking the sexiest lines. Ecstasy was claiming leadership as its sales increased 323 percent during 1982 (53). In 1984, Harlequin's sensual Temptation line was launched to compete, but still the company was spending advertising on its brand-name rather than on its authors or the sexiness of its new line. The new, more selective readers ignored brand-name and bought by author and degree of sensuality. Loveswept, which emphasized authors and depended for promotion on word-of-mouth, was an immediate hit in 1984 (54).

But the war of the categories was over. First, because "the sexy angle . . . was losing its luster," even as Dell launched its Ecstasy Supreme in 1983 and Bantam its "author's line" in 1984. Readers

had begun seeking alternate forms of romance, especially historical romances and regencies, and some readers even turned to traditional mysteries. By 1984, returns of unsold romances were as
high as 70 percent for both Harlequin Enterprises Limited and
Silhouette Books (55).

Second, in August 1984 came the headline: "S & S to Distribute
Harlequin, Silhouette." The fight was over; Silhouette Books, using literary agents and publicity consultants, had set out to determine what American women "really wanted to read," and its sales
had eclipsed Harlequin's (50).

Total sales continued lower than their peak in 1983. Nevertheless, in 1986 romances still formed the bulk of women's book
purchases and women bought 59 percent of all books sold. Wom-
en's purchases consisted of 49 percent fiction and 38 percent non-
fiction, with romances making up 22 percent of their fiction purchases (Wood, 1987: 27).

The "romance war" increased attention to the women's romance phenomenon, but as early as 1980 interested scholars had
already begun to ask: what do American women want to read and
why do so many read romances? The readers themselves said: "it's
escape," "a vacation," "the only thing that's mine," "we need
outlets," "courting was the best time of my life," "I totally believe
it's therapy." And scholars and other experts agreed, adding: "Many
[readers] find [a romance] a helpful antidote to the increasing stress
in their lives, particularly as they have entered the labor force while
trying to keep up with home and family responsibilities." Thurston wrote that many readers "obtain information about history,
about various careers . . . about sex. . . . They want to learn
about the kinds of relationships that other women develop with
their sexual partners, and they want to know how they behave in
them" (Thurston, 1983: 14).

Although the new romances were often designated "porn for
women," their readers still eschewed the kind of pornography
written for men, preferring language that veiled sexual encounters.
Janice A. Radway discovered in her study of readers that they
"seem to dislike any kind of detailed description of male geni-
talia" (Radway, 1983: 64). And Kathryn Falk pointed out, "Romance readers don't want to read of the sex act in graphic

terms. . . . You will not find the words *penis, cunnilingus, sodomy*, or any textbook term in a category romance" (Falk, 1983: 113). On the other hand even these concerns could change. Alice Morgan, author, had this to say of readers' preference: "I have received no letters from readers offended by *im*plicit amatory liasons, though many have requested increased *ex*plicitness and frequency" (125). No one was more to the point than Donna Kimel Vitek, author of fourteen category romances, who wrote, "The captivated reader actually feels the rush of desire . . . experienced by the characters" (118).

Readers were not ciphers. They realized romances were escape literature but insisted they learned from them (Radway, 1983: 59). Still, publishers—notably Harlequin—mistakenly thought readers bought by brand name rather than selectively. In 1978, Dave Sanderson, Harlequin's former director of marketing, said, "All titles sell about evenly" (Maryles, 1978: 376). Barbara Rudolph (writing for *Forbes*, March 1982), couldn't quite come to disagreement with Sanderson but pointed out: "Confronted with an excess of choice, readers may resort to buying books based on author, title or cover. So far, that shows no signs of happening" (Rudolph, 1982: 51).

In summer of 1981, in my rural locale, sales of new Harlequin Romances and Presents, the sexier Harlequin line, showed that some readers grabbed all six new Harlequin Presents as they arrived each month. But it was also apparent that some readers refused to buy Harlequins written by specific authors who wrote with a minimum of sensuality.

Others close to readers agreed with this observation. In 1983, ten Romance Mavens found that their customers "are currently buying more by author than imprint." One of the Mavens, Barbara Wren, "noted that many of her customers who had been ordering Harlequin and Silhouette romance via mail order are discontinuing the service." They wanted to buy by author (Maryles, 1983: 54).

By 1983, the most popular authors, with the exception of Barbara Cartland, wrote sensual romances. Harlequin Enterprises Limited was late to understand this trend. Its American market share remained high in 1982, 58 percent, with two million sales (Maryles, 1983: 54). But beginning in 1980, Harlequin got far more unsold book returns than anticipated. "Harlequin is a classic case of missing out on a changing market. Its staple was innocent love, but readers gradually developed an appetite for less naive heroines and spicier plots" (Rudolph, 1982: 50). Barbara Rudolph went on to note that Dell's sexy Candlelight Ecstasy line, begun in December 1980, was followed by Jove's steamy Second Chance at Love and that Silhouette Books' Desire was initiated in June 1982. Another tamer line faltered; Terry Brombeck—market manager of Bantam's Circle of Love, introduced March 1982—said, "We got caught in a marketplace that quickly shifted, with the readers wanting more sensual and believable plots" (Maryles, 1983: 56).

Some lines were even more responsive to readers. For example, Loveswept featured mini-profiles and photographs of its authors, and supplied plots that were "highly sexual," according to Carolyn Nichols, their editor. This new line avoided overworked plots; for example, marriages of convenience, an old staple device, were out (Rudolph, 1983: 55). Other new lines such as Rapture Romances, featured "more romance, more passion, a strong and capable woman—and a hero who is not a macho-bully," said Maryanne Palumbo, publicity director of New American Library (56).

This growing sexuality was seen by some analysts as positive; "Today's romance readers see nothing pornographic about sex when it's a part of love, which is the way it's being portrayed" (Thurston, 1983: 15). On the other hand, as long ago as 1979 and 1980, feminists like Ann Douglas were expressing concern that the new romances constituted mindless pornography for women.

3

Feminist Studies of Women's Popular Romances

Ann Douglas, writing in 1980, noted that in romances "the strong woman seldom fares well, or if she does it is at man's expense, and thus at her own" (Douglas, 1980: 25). She labeled much of popular culture designed for women "soft-core pornography" and noted the Harlequin romance novels as a popular type of this pornography. She pointed out, "The timing of the Harlequins' prodigious success [in the 1970s] has coincided exactly with the appearance and spread of the women's movement, and much of its increasingly anti-feminist content reflects this symbiotic relationship" (26).

Douglas noted the punishing behavior of heroes of Harlequin romance novels and the over-responsiveness of the heroines to the heroes, and concluded about their relationships, "The Harlequins are porn softened to fit the needs of female emotionality. They are located inside the female consciousness." Further, "Harlequins are dramas of dependency" (27–28).

Douglas's 1980 conclusions formed important insights into the sexier Harlequins published from 1973 to 1980, when some Harlequin Romances were steamy while some were not. However, romances by American authors of Harlequin American Romances, Silhouette Books, Second Chance at Loves, and so forth, departed in significant ways from those earlier Harlequin romance novels written by British authors. Were these newer category romances still "dramas of dependency" and so forth?

Recently, disagreeing that Harlequin Romances were pornography for women, Tania Modleski took a psychoanalytical approach to them, gothics (romantic mysteries in which a wife often worries that her husband wants her dead), and American soap operas. Harlequin Romances constituted the only category romances in the 1970s, and Modleski saw them as covert expressions of female rage. According to her observations, based on Harlequin Romances published from 1970 to the early 1980s, readers identified with heroines who rebelled against their own helplessness, insofar as it was engendered by the power and authority of modern men. She found that the three types of narrative she studied dealt with women's deep-rooted anxieties and repressive fantasies. In the real world, Modleski pointed out, a woman is compromised as she tries to be herself but also tries to see herself as men see her. A Harlequin Romance enhanced this double consciousness as the observer-reader identified with its heroine. In addition, she found that Harlequin Romances appealed to repressive fantasies which relied on readers' memories of infancy, when they were protected and cherished (Modleski, 1982: 29–32).

However, Modleski argued that Harlequin Romances were also narratives that contained elements of women's protest and resistance. An important aspect of their world was that the hero was cruel to the heroine in order to mask his love for her. Thus "male brutality comes to be seen as a manifestation not of contempt, but of love" (41). But while men's brutality was explained, the novels had to "somehow provide an outlet for female resentment" of that male brutality. Modleski found that reader satisfaction derived from elements of a revenge fantasy as, in the end of the romance, the hero was brought to his knees by his love for the heroine (45).

Modleski saw these Harlequin Romances as constituting a subversive force in patriarchal society (see also Mussell, 1984: 19–20). Female rage was tempered, however. At the end of the romances, the heroine turned against her better self—that is, her independent self which was angry at men's power and authority—in order to join with the hero in monogamous, patriarchal marriage (Modleski, 1982: 14). Therefore, Modleski dubbed the Harlequin Romance "the hysterical text" pointing out that the reader found herself "desiring the subversion of the heroine's attempts at self-assertion" in order to attain a happy ending, defined as that kind of marriage (33).

According to Eileen Fallon, Modleski found "that female power is the real concern" of Harlequin Romances, as it is of the gothic romance and soap opera genres which Modleski also studied (Fallon, 1984: 57). However, Modleski studied only Harlequin Romances and did not note either the other category lines which emerged beginning in December 1980 or the changes in Harlequin Romances after 1980 (58).

Even before Modleski's book was published, Ann Barr Snitow asked another important question. "Between readers and publishers[,] who is manipulating whom" (Snitow, 1979: 142)? She added,

The mass audience may be . . . capable of digesting contradictory cultural impulses and at the same time resisting suggestion altogether. . . . I observe in [Harlequin Romances] neither an effective top down propaganda effort against women's liberation, nor a covert flowering of female sexuality. Instead, I see them as accurate descriptions of certain *selected* elements of female consciousness (143).

I am in agreement; people are not what they read.

Turning from reader to product, Snitow pointed out that the heroines were portrayed as ordinary women, but that their every action was sexual. The hero was attracted by that sexuality and went on to notice how helpful the heroine was to him; heroines always supported men's egos and projects. While the heroines were helpful, heroes of Harlequin Romances were thoroughly nasty. As Snitow rightly pointed out, the happy endings, "the thirty page denouement[s were] powerless to dispel the earlier impression of [his] menace." As did Modleski, Snitow noted that Harlequin "offers the impossible" (146), the hero's brutality as a manifestation of his love. To Modleski's theory of the divided self, Snitow added that heroines lied constantly about their sexual desires in order to protect their reputations (148).

Why, then, were romances so popular? Snitow wrote, "When women try to imagine companionship, [American] society offers . . . male, sexual companionship. . . When women try to fantasize about sex, the society offers them taboos on most of its imaginable expressions except those that deal directly with arousing and satisfying men" (149). Furthermore,

> Harlequin romances make bridges between contradictions; they soothe ambivalence. A brutal male sexuality [in a world of short marriages and frequent rapes] is magically converted to romance. . . . Stereotyped female roles are charged with an unlikely glamor. . . . Independence is always presented as a mere counter in the sexual game, like a hairdo . . . ; sexual feeling utterly defeats its early stirrings (150–51).

Finally, Snitow pointed to the power of the heroines of Harlequin Romances and their reward. She found Harlequins to be women's pornography in which the heroine was anxious to "control the flow of sexual passion between herself and the hero until her surrender can be on her own terms" (158).

While Snitow, Douglas, and Modleski studied Harlequin Romances, this study adds the newer category romance lines and relies on a study of best-selling romances. It therefore augments Kay Mussell's 1984 work on women's romance fiction.

Mussell's important book, *Fantasy and Reconciliation: Contemporary Formulas of Women's Romance Fiction*, details the history of romances in western culture, explores uses of settings and women's roles in those romances, and asks why women read romances. She was impressed that while sex was important in the novels of the early 1980s,

> The essential assumptions of romance formulas—belief in the primacy of love in a woman's life, female passivity in romantic relationships, support for monogamy in marriage, reinforcement of domestic values—have not faded or significantly altered (Mussell, 1984: xii).

Mussell also concerned herself with possible pornographic elements in these newer romances and found that "even today, sex remains ethereal and emotional, rarely physical or prurient. . . . [The heroine] *receives* sexual experience from the hero instead of actively participating. . . . Sexuality serves the plot's development instead of dominating it" (128).

In some ways, as Mussell noted, newer category romances followed the lead of best-selling mass market and trade romances.

Carol Thurston studied these kinds of historical romances and other bestsellers. She said of 56 historicals published 1978 through 1981,

Certainly the sexual activity of heroines before marriage [depicted in these books] describes contemporary society more accurately than [the Victorian period, a common setting for these stories]. . . . [The] heroine . . . ultimately becomes a kind of superwoman—passionate lover, friend and confidante to her husband, devoted mother, and astute businesswoman with a social conscience (Thurston, 1985: 43; see also Thurston and Doscher, 1982: 49–51).

By 1977–1978, best-sellers were explicity sexual and sexual scenes were liberally sprinkled throughout many of them. This continued to be true in 1981–1982 as category romances grew spicier; however, these more recent best-sellers veered away from the 1977–1978 craze for portraying heroes raping heroines, and toward an incest fad. This shift indicated that authors and publishers knew their market and realized that women readers found rape disagreeable. As Falk noted, "Readers' protestations of rape scenes have cut back on the violence in 'bodice rippers' " (Falk, 1983: 5). Authors and publishers also realized that readers wanted titillation and tried incest as a new sexual taboo to explore. Like other such fads, incest was soon replaced.

In a raging market, once mass paperback romances portraying pre-marital sex began to sell widely, category romances began to portray pre-marital sex. The first such Harlequin Presents encountered in this study was Anne Mather's *images of love*, published December 1980. (The titles of Harlequin Presents are in lower case in order to throw their authors' names into prominence.) It may be vital to note that Anne Mather was Harlequin's most productive author by 1980.

As best-sellers became more erotic, Janice A. Radway began the most intriguing study of romances to date. Rather than focusing on the texts, Radway studied romance readers and their responses to romances. She used "developments in semiotics, reader-response criticism, Russian formalism, ethnographic anthropology, and feminist cultural analysis" (Allen, 1985: 185) to study 42 women readers residing in Smithton, Pennsylvania, in 1980 and 1981.

Radway followed Nancy Chodorow's feminist theories. A cursory summation: like sons, a daughter's first emotional relationship is most often with her mother. Faced with her mother's preference for a man, the maturing daughter experiences penis envy, identifies with her father, and admires men and boys as she asserts her independence from her mother (Radway, 1984: 136). Thus the daughter carries an "internal emotional triangle" into adulthood—mother, self, and men. Since most men are less nurturant than mother, they do not entirely displace her. That is, they do not fulfill the adult daughter's need for nurturance (137). In the "ideal romance" however, the hero is a man who knows how to nurture a heroine (140) and thus replace the triangle with a dyad (also see Chodorow, 1978).

Radway's readers differentiated the ideal romance from the "failed romance" and from the many romances which fell between these categories. According to them, an ideal romance hero, although spectacularly masculine—i.e., having very high social status and being extremely heterosexual—was nurturant. That is, he gave the heroine verbal assurances of his love, was tender, and combined "fatherly protection, motherly care, and passionate adult love" (Radway, 131–49). Heroes of failed romances were unrelievedly masculine: aggressive but not tender, socially and economically independent but never emotionally dependent, reserved at all times and never verbally emotional (168).

Radway concluded by noting that readers sought ideal romances "not out of [their personal] contentment but out of dissatisfaction, longing, and protest" against their patriarchal world (215). In addition, she pointed out that romances rested on the assumption that heterosexuality and monogamous marriage constituted a heroine's only sexual choices. Based on these assumptions, the ideal romance provided its readers with a strategy by which to reinterpret their own relationships with men (15). Furthermore, a romance "function[ed] as a utopian wish-fulfillment fantasy" in which the heroine, and the reader identifying with her, acquired "an exclusive and intense emotional relationship with a tender, life-giving individual" (151).

Radway's text sources were the historical and contemporary romances designated by her readers. (Historicals are set in the past; contemporaries, in the present. In her study, both types were published since 1970.) Thus, Radway's readers preferred romances, often designated "paperback best-sellers", to category romances. However, by 1982 the most popular romances were category romances, not best-sellers.

This was largely because by 1982 category romances had changed their portrayal of sexuality. Furthermore, between 1970 and 1987, with the introduction of ever increasing numbers of American authors, category romances shifted away from themes characteristic of the failed "best-seller" romances studied by Radway—and the Harlequin Romances studied by Modleski—towards those of the ideal romances desired by Radway's readers. Therefore, a study of the changes in category romances reinforces many of Radway's conclusions about reader preference.

However, noting Sandra M. Gilbert's contention that Radway's work "may . . . suffer from an apparently diligent empiricism that sometimes masks speculation" (Gilbert, 1984: 11) and taking into account conversations with Radway, who dismisses the idea that the real concern of romances is women's power, this study will show that the power relationship between protagonists has shifted in recent category romances. The hero has become not only more nurturant but also less macho, and the heroine has turned sexually lusty and less passive in general. As noted above, Anne Gisonny, executive editor of Candlelight Ecstasy, cautioned American writers to avoid always assigning dominance to heroes and passive victimization to heroines.

By 1987, Carol Thurston could note that in romances "the strong, independent heroine now is simply assumed (Thurston, April, 1987: 12). Reviewers of romances agreed and "saw a rise in the heroines's intelligence level." They added that romance heroes were "sensitive, caring men . . . [who] are allowed to need the heroine in ways other than sexual" (Kolaczyk, 1987: 42–43). These reader-reviewers pointed out that "Over the past five years [1982–1987] . . . [sex] has gotten more and more explicit. Too much so . . . for much of it seems gratuitous." Furthermore, they emphasized, "Nothing turns the reviewers off a book faster than violence disguised as lovemaking" (43). As will be seen, this study will indicate that American readers have manipulated American publishers of romances at least as much as those publishers have manipulated their readers.

But other questions arise. Were these newer romances, written by American authors, still dramas of dependency involving helpful heroines and nasty heroes? Did these romances still soothe ambivalence? Were they repressive fantasies? Were their heroines using independence as a mere ploy? Did they still feature heroines hiding their sexual impulses? Were heroes brought to their knees by the sexual power of the heroines? Were these newer romances increasingly anti-feminist? Were they pornographic? All these questions are refinements of earlier ones: What rewards do today's romances offer unliberated American women and are those rewards changing? What do these romances tell us about American women's fears of fully empowered women?

4

Harlequin Romances and Presents 1970 Through 1982: Category Romances Written by United Kingdom Authors

The originator and the model for formula romance is the Harlequin Romance. Canada-based Harlequin Enterprises Limited began publication in May 1949. Among the early titles published were reprints of books from Mills & Boon, a British publisher that began publishing romance novels shortly after its formation in 1907. Harlequin and Mills & Boom merged in 1972. The earliest products were labeled Romances and, as Harlequin Enterprises Limited responded to its consumers' changing interests, this line was joined in May 1973 by Harlequin Presents. The Presents line highlights authors and was meant to be "more dramatic and more sophisticated" than the Romance line (*Thirty Years*, 1979: 95). By 1984, Harlequin published five lines: Romance, Presents (both averaged 190 pages in length), Superromance (a longer 380-page romance), American Romance (250 pages), and Temptation (220 pages).

These romance lines are particularly interesting products for the student of popular culture because, as Dave Sanderson, the former director of marketing for Harlequin Enterprises Limited said in 1978, "There is almost nothing Harlequin does without consumer research and testing in the marketplace" (Maryles, 1978: 375–76). But, as noted above, this marketplace testing failed to alert the leader of category romance publishing to the swift change in reader preference between 1980 and 1983.

This overconfidence rested on enormous sales. According to Fred

Kerner, former vice-president of publishing in the Toronto Office of Harlequin Enterprises Limited, in 1980 the corporation sold 188 million English language volumes. Sixty to sixty-five percent of these were sold in the United States, and these figures did not include library circulation or used book sales. Furthermore, these romances were published in 14 languages and sold in 90 countries by 1980 (16th Harlequin Party, 1980).

As an added note of interest, almost all Harlequin authors—except those writing Harlequin American Romances—are British, a few live in Canada, Australia, New Zealand, and South Africa. By contrast, bestselling romances as well as later category romances sold in the United States are usually written by American women.

Who bought and read Harlequin Romances and Presents? In 1980, the majority of the British readers (and probably of the American readers) were married women between the ages of 25 and 54, with readership tapering off after age 45 (Mussell, 1980: 7). These readers are of special interest in this study, because while unmarried women might aspire to tradition—as defined in the introduction—married women between the ages of 25 and 45 often tried to live the traditional role.

The most intriguing question in popular culture is, why do people consume it? In this case, why did married women read these novels when Harlequin Romances and Presents, like most bestselling romances written by women, were not about married life? Instead, they centered on courtship. Did Harlequin Romances and Presents make women's traditional role appear more attractive through its treatment of courtship?

Harlequin Enterprises Limited itself (through its former representatives like Sanderson) said, "Like men's adventure fiction, Harlequin romances are pure and simple escape." Furthermore, Sanderson believed they were addictive. "We don't have to have a 'pay off' on a single title. We know that once we get a reader hooked she comes back for more" ("Harlequin Launches," 1975: 38). This was the broadly accepted view until the early 1980s. However, readers became more selective than Harlequin Enterprises Limited thought they were in 1975, even as significant numbers became addicted to reading romances. While reader addiction is not studied here, it is explored in Janice Radway's study of readers.

Kay Mussell found, in 1980, that readers were "remarkably inarticulate about their pleasure in [Harlequin Romances]" and this study agrees. However, as Mussell noted, "I have never been convinced by what [readers] say" (Mussell, 1980: 1). Readers of all category fiction always say, "I read a——for escape." In her *Fantasy and Reconciliation: Contemporary Formulas of Women's Romance Fiction*, Mussell argued that, "All [category] fiction provides *escape from* present reality; the choice of formula allows *escape to* a world that appears more satisfactory than the readers' own" (Mussell, 1984: 11).

What underlies this reading for escape? One student of women's romances, Kate Ellis (then associate professor of English at Rutgers University's Livingston College) wrote, "Women fantasize about how to acquire power. The fantasy is that it can be gotten through marriage" (O'Toole, 1979: 65). And courtship is the process by which a woman may contract a powerful marriage. As Joanna Russ said, "The Love Story is—for women—*bildungsroman*, success, failure, education, and the only adventure possible, all in one" (Russ, 1978: 298). But while there is merit in these views, Patricia O'Toole suggested that market research may prove that these romances sell, and yet it has not been able to draw a portrait of their typical reader (O'Toole, 1979: 64). Nor has market research been able to tell us why women read Harlequin Romances or any category romances. For answers to these questions, feminist researchers like Radway and Tania Modleski must be consulted.

The thesis here, as noted above, agrees that readers have found these courtship novels to be relaxing power fantasies of the woman's great adventure. Furthermore, readers have also found in them guidelines for living and, at least until 1980, assurances that the traditional woman's role was rewarding. On this point, I am seconded by other students of popular culture. For example, Will Wright said,

The narrative structure [of popular fiction] offers a model of socialization by presenting identifiable social types and showing how they interact. The receivers of the [model] learn how to act by recognizing their own situation in it and observing how it is resolved (Wright, 1975: 186).

Ray B. Browne quoted Ross Macdonald, "We learn to see reality through the popular arts we create and patronize. That's what they're for. That's why we love them" (Browne, 1978: 15–16).

Since many of the readers were married women, the hypothesis here is that Harlequin Romances gave them guidelines on how to cope with man-woman relationships, and that their heroines coped in basically traditional ways. More specifically, the reader was receiving guidelines on how to handle marriage to a stranger in a world in which women and men were not only socialized to be as different as possible from each other, but also to have very different expectations of marriage (Bernard, 1973). Thus, Harlequin Romances offered an explanation of and a cure for the frustrations of middle-class marriage in the 1970s. They delineated men and women who were very different from each other, hence strangers, and declared that a heterosexual couple could come together only when a woman and a man loved each other and could communicate that love to each other.

Along with guidelines, Harlequin Romances furnished readers with myths. The major myth was romantic love. By the 1970s, American mythic romantic love triumphed over all and any differences between men and women, came once in a lifetime, and lasted until death. Romantic love joined dominant, powerful heroes—protectors—with morally superior, nurturant heroines—who were in need of protection.

Since all Harlequin Romances and Presents centered on romantic love, which ones to work with was a basic question. The most important discovery Melanie Kahleck made in her study of Harlequins was that they became ever sexier during the 1970s (Kahleck, 1980). The present study concentrated on the works of the "sexier" authors and, as shown in *Thirty Years of Harlequins*, the authors used in this research include all but 3 of the most productive Harlequin Romance and Presents authors (1979). Those were not included because Jane Arbor, Joyce Dingwell, and Jean S. MacLeod had not published any Harlequin Presents. Many of the authors used here were new in 1980 and 3 of them—Ann Cooper, Carole Mortimer, and Janet Dailey—had published only Harlequin Presents. Their writings were among the most sexually suggestive of the romances used here and represented the new trend. At the other end of the scale was the work of the long popular "tame 2," Mary Burchell and Betty Neels. These authors included no overtly sensual scenes in their novels, and, when their protagonists kissed, the kiss was scarcely provocative: " 'Darling—' he took her face between his hands and kissed her on the lips" (Burchell, 1980: 183).

Tamer Harlequin Romances were still published as late as 1986. Presumably, these were meant to keep elements of the old audience who still preferred "G rated" category romances.

How did readers differentiate between the steamy and the bland? In the late 1970s and early 1980s, "sexier" in a Harlequin Romance or Presents meant a lot of sexual punishment.

Reading the come-on blurbs which appeared on the outside covers of 21 randomly selected 1970 Harlequin Romances, none of them emphasized sexuality. These constituted 21 percent of the 96 published in 1970. (The 1970 Harlequin Romances did not have inside promotional blurbs.) In contrast, in the 1978–1980 sample—appraising the outside cover and the inside promotional blurb where both were available—2 of the outside covers of the sample (15 of the steamier novels) emphasized sexuality, and one of them punishing sexualty, Violet Winspear's *the sheik's captive*: "For when the Sheik learned her identity he planned to use Diane to wreak vengeance on her grandfather, his longtime enemy. By violating her chastity he would make her grandfather suffer!" (1979). For the purpose of this chapter, a sexy Harlequin Romance or Presents was one that involved such punishment. While some of the books had erotic sections—that is, segments depicting non-violent sexuality—here were none in the sample which had such sections unaccompanied by scenes involving sexual punishment.

None of the 1970 sample covers involved even a kiss. By contrast, of the 1978–1980 sample of 17, 13 (or 77 percent) had inside blurbs that alluded to sexuality. Many of these involved a kiss (10 of the 15 sexier books). An example from one of the not especially heated but not sexually subdued, Margaret Pargeter's *A Man Called Cameron*: "He took her lips slowly, lingeringly, with a punishing sweetness" (1978).

In all the risqué Romances, punishing sexuality arose from antagonism between the stranger-hero and the stranger-heroine. Therefore, I looked for a rising level of such antagonism between the 1970 and the 1978–1980 samples. Whereas the 1970 sample indicated antagonism between heroine and hero in 38 percent of the Romances, in the 1978–1980 Romances and Desires antagonism was indicated in 9 of 15 outside blurbs (or 60 percent) and in 10 of 13 that had inside blurbs (or 77 percent). If potential readers had judged both the inside and outside blurbs, they would have found that 13 of the 15 sexier novels indicated antagonism. The blurbs for the 2 tame novels were similar to those found in the 1970 sample; there were no kisses and only one indicated muted antagonism.

These changes in Harlequin Romances and Desires reflected societal change. During the 1960s, the number of American women and girls engaging in premarital sex increased markedly, and this trend continued during the 1970s (Tavris and Offir, 1977: 65). For example, statistics reported in 1981, in the *New York Times*, in a report by Nadine Brozan entitled "Teenage Pregnancy: The Problem that Hasn't Gone Away": "Of the 29 million people aged 13 to 19, 12 million—7 million boys and 5 million girls—have had sexual intercourse." By the age of 19, two-thirds of American females had had sexual intercourse (Brozan, 1981: 17–19). As the United States experienced this social change, so did England and other United Kingdom countries.

Nevertheless, Harlequin Romances and Presents continued to deal with basically virginal females. This was true in 1970 and it was still true in all but one of the 1978–80 sample. But the newer, more heated Romances and Presents evidenced an important shift while continuing to sell the virginal aspect of the traditional woman's role. The nineteenth–century unmarried woman was supposed to be uninterested in sexuality, and the virgins in the 1970s Harlequin Romances seemed uninterested. In contrast, the virgins in the 1978–1980 Romances and Presents lusted, and their lust was not only central to the plot but, as noted above, the major reason for the rising popularity of Harlequin Romances and Presents among American readers. While these heroines lusted, it is important to point out that like most fiction directed at women, and in contrast to most fiction directed at men, Harlequin heroines still basically rejected premarital sex. (For example, in 1975, Dwayne Smith and Marc Marte discovered in their study—comparing 48 women's romance magazine stories with 27 men's adventure magazine stories—that 76 percent of the romance stories rejected pre- and extramarital sex, while 100 percent of the adventure stories upheld them (Smith and Marte, 1975: 309–15).

To add randomness to the 1978–1980 sample, five Harlequin

Presents issued June 1982 were added. Their covers were less erotic than those of some of the other category lines popular in 1982, and similar to earlier Presents covers. Four of their blurbs indicated antagonism between their protagonists, and four involved punishing kisses.

Turning to the stories themselves, what did Harlequin Romances and Presents, published 1978–1982, say to their readers?

THE HARLEQUIN ROMANCES AND PRESENTS

> Initial hostility, fear even, had turned to blinding love (Carole Mortimer, *savage interlude*: 98).

The Romances, until the late 1970s, involved low-status, virginal, young (averaging 19 1/2 years old) heroines who attracted older (10 to even 20 years older), high-status heroes. In the late 1970s, most Romances and Desires featured virginal heroines who lusted after sexually experienced, older, increasingly brutal, and ever higher-status heroes. Their liaisons were not sexually consummated until after marriage.

By 1980–1982, however, almost half of the heroines had sexual intercourse with the heroes before marriage. Nevertheless, this newer model of the "virgin" heroine was monogamous and eventually married the only man with whom she had ever experienced sexual intercourse. So, as rival category romances written by American women featured pre-marital sex, this eventually constituted a trend in Harlequin as well.

The structure of these novels was not significantly different from the earlier Harlequin Romances studied by Kay Mussell. She wrote, "They are, in fact, much more alike than any other kind of formula fiction I know, except perhaps pornography. . . . Girl meets man; problems (mostly of their own making) keep them apart; they come to an understanding and happiness" (Mussell, 1980: 3).

To further elaborate Mussell's point, in 1978–1982 Harlequin Romances and Presents, heroes ("men") and heroines ("girls") met as strangers. Very different from each other, they were strange to each other as well. Heroines usually trembled and tripped around heroes who were powerful and "sardonic" (the operative word). Furthermore in this sample, only one hero and heroine grew up together and they had been parted for years as the novel began (Charlotte Lamb, *call back yesterday*, 1978). At first meeting, the heroine and hero usually disliked one another. In the sexier novels, however, mutual sexual attraction occurred instantly. And while in many of these sexier novels a secondary man was liked by the heroine, who disliked the hero—and the hero was most often thoroughly unlikable—the hero won the heroine in the end because he was a "real man." That is, the hero was as different as possible from the secondary man and, especially, from the heroine.

The protagonists' dislike combined with their mutual attraction, either gave rise to "problems," or their antagonism was compounded by problems that here are labelled misunderstandings. That is, the hero and heroine, strange to each other, had communication difficulties. The solution to these misunderstandings was the protagonists' admitted love for each other. After that admission—and getting each to admit her or his love was the crux of these romances—the protagonists could marry and have children or their marriage could be consummated and happy. (Of the 24 books studied, four involved marriages in which the heroine was forced by her hero to marry him, and one other involved an unconsummated though mutually entered marriage—Daphne Clair, *the loving trap*, 1982).

THE HEROES

"Men all over . . . stubborn as a mule, but that helpless" (Lamb, *dark dominion*, 1980: 137).

Like most men novelists who depict female protagonists as unrealistic others, according to Elaine Showalter, seldom do women novelists portray realistic heroes. This is not only true of the authors of Harlequin Romances and Presents, it is also true of women who write popular literature as well as best sellers and other brands of category romances. And, as Showalter pointed out, this has been true since British and American women began publishing novels.

She found that most nineteenth-century British women authors depicted heroes who were not whole people but "either angels or devils" (Showalter, 1977: 134). In the sexier Harlequin Romances and Presents, 1978–1982 heroes were devils or at least devilish, never angels. In this respect, they were fundamentally differentiated from virginal heroines, who were only slightly more "real" than their heroes.

The devilish heroes in these romances were also strangers, designed to appeal to women's fantasies. As Nancy Friday and Karen Shanor discovered, American women frequently fantasized about male strangers. Friday pointed out that this was so because, "Anonymity frees a woman to take what she's always wanted sexually" (Friday, 1973: 93; see also Shanor, 1977). This chapter underscores that finding.

The heroes, then, were strange, incomprehensible but fascinating others. To the heroines, they were so difficult to understand that they seemed to have split personalities. Primarily, this effect was conveyed by contrasting the heroes' sardonic behavior and sneer with their gentleness and smile. Secondarily, this schizophrenia was shown by contrasting the hard-driving hero (when he was at work) to the tender hero (when paired with animals or with people other than the heroine). Thus, the potential husband-father (provider and protector) was the alter ego side of the stranger. It became the heroine's job to reconcile the two.

There was no hemming or hawing about the heroes as sardonic, brutish devils. Some of their names were marvelously malevolent. My favorite was Devil Haggard, who was paired with Oriel Millstock in Charlotte Lamb's *call back yesterday*. But there were others like Damien Savage, coupled with Kate Darwood, in Carole Mortimer's *savage interlude*. Obviously, the titles themselves were often suggestive of savagery and furthermore of obsession, as in Lamb's *dark dominion*, Yvonne Whittal's *Bitter Enchantment*, Ann Cooper's *battle with desire*, and Clair's *the loving trap*. And, as will be seen, these sensual romances were about obsession—the heroine's obsession with the hero—but, primarily, his obsession with her; opposites attracting through mutual fixation.

The adjectives applied to the hero, especially when he was introduced, were telling. On the first page of Violet Winspear's *love is the honey*, the hero was "so alarmingly foreign" that "the look of the man stayed in [the heroine's] mind" (Winspear, 1980: 5). Introducing the hero of Sally Wentworth's *Liberated Lady*, "The stranger strode purposefully . . . looming over and glaring at her" (Wentworth, 1979: 14). Portraying the most egalitarian couple in all of the books cited in this chapter, Rachel Lindsay wrote in *love and no marriage*, "The voice [of the hero] was very definitely male . . . deep and dark brown . . . But . . . another underlying color. Black, perhaps." "A tone of growing impatience" was noted as their first conversation progressed (Lindsay, 1980: 31–32).

Frequently, but not always, the man at work, a thorough stranger to his heroine who did not understand him or his work, best exhibited his non-husband side. The prime example came from Lamb's *dark dominion*, in which the hero was a barrister. "She had once been to see [James at] work. . . . The tall, white-wigged stranger standing there had been a nightmare figure to her. It had been after that, she realized, that she had grown frightened of him. He had begun to use his court voice on her, his tone cold and clear, his eyes penetrating. She had responded by shrinking from him" (Lamb, 1980: 40).

In contrast was the warm side of the hero, the hero with animals and other people. In Whittal's *Bitter Enchantment*, the heroine presented the hero to her grandmother. "Melanie stared in amazement at the transformation in the man standing beside her. With his austere features relaxed into a genuine smile" (Whittal, 1979: 35). Earlier in the novel, Whittal presented her hero as having a "cold glance [that] swept over [the heroine] disdainfully, and [whose] hard mouth twisted derisively" (7). In Lamb's *a frozen fire*, Mark's niece "and dog went across the room in a great tidal rush and both ended up attached with loving enthusiasm to him. Over their heads [the hero] grinned at Helen" (Lamb, 1980: 93). Mark, the nicest hero in the sample, began the story as a "great dark bulk passing rapidly," "a figure of primitive fury" (5–6).

Their warm sides assured readers that these schizoid heroes had the makings of good family men. And in these novels a heroine could and did integrate her hero's two personalities, after which he emerged as husband and potential father. As one of Anne Mather's heroines thought, "the two men she had known [were] Robert Lang; and to her eternal shame she knew an urgent desire to fuse the two halves into one" (Mather, 1980: 94).

The schizophrenic, sarcastic, strange hero was further distanced from his heroine by his size (six-feet-two seemed popular) and his wealth (there wasn't a poor man in the sample, although the hero of the tame *Nightingales* by Burchell was a mere famous choirmaster in one of England's large churches; and Alex Gantry/Leon Graham was less wealthy than Olivia Gantry (Mather, 1982). In the steamier novels, the heroes were rich or famous or both and, with two exceptions (Rachel Lindsay, *love and no marriage*, 1980 and Mather, *smokescreen*, 1982) had higher status than the heroines. For example, Janet Bauling's hero, an internationally famous newscaster, fell in love with a college student (Bauling, 1982); in Anne Cooper's *battle with desire*, the heroine, a budding violinist, lusted after a world-famous conductor. The most widely divergent couple was Iris Ardath, who was about to become a nun, and Zonar Mavrakis, the Onassis-like, self-made, Greek tycoon in Winspear's *love is the honey*.

In addition, as also noted by Mussell, the age differences reinforced the heroes' dominance. In the 1978–1980 sample, the youngest heroine was 17 to her hero's 34 (Mortimer, 1980). The closest age difference occurred in Lamb's *call back yesterday*, in which the heroine was the oldest of all the heroines, 29. She was a widow with one son and her hero, with whom she grew up, seemed to be her age. The age differences, where stated, varied from a low of 7 years to a high of 20. In the 1982 sample, the average age of the heroine was 22 and the average difference in ages was over 13 years.

As if all these traits weren't enough, the heroes were portrayed as elegant and experienced—that is, worldly in general, but primarily sexually knowing. They were often labelled "womanizers" and sharply contrasted with their inelegant and virginal heroines. This was conveyed first by bluntly telling the reader it was so. Even in Sally Wentworth's *Liberated Lady*, in which the heroine was a junior executive in advertising and a 26-year-old virgin, the hero was not only "tall, about six feet two . . . with broad shoulders . . . lean, almost autocratic features. Features that were set in an angry frown as he looked at her sardonically from his grey eyes" (Wentworth, 1979: 14). He was also, "Too clever and knowledgeable about women by half" (97).

Second, as already noted, the hero's differentness, as well as his power and dominance, were conveyed through formulaic adjectives (sardonic, steely). Further, the protagonists were introduced by stressing their differences through contrasting phrases, as in Yvonne Whittal's *Bitter Enchantment*. The heroine had "delicate features," and the hero "had looked right through her with such intensity that . . . she had felt strangely breathless" (Whittal, 1979: 5–6).

Not only were the sexes different—he experienced; she naive—at times the authors sharpened the difference by stylistically undermining their heroines while aggrandizing the heroes. For example, Whittal in her cliché-ridden novel *Bitter Enchantment* subverted her heroine as follows: " 'I won't be blackmailed into bed with you, Jason,' "—here the heroine showed some strength, but then the author added, "she remarked tritely after a reflective pause" (118). Contrast her treatment by the hero: " 'Shut up!' he grunted, silencing her eloquently with his mouth" (124).

Then there is the heroes' psychic superiority. Women are supposed to be the perceptive sex, and frequently the heroines have been able to read between the lines. But in all but one case, *love and no marriage*, the hero was more perceptive than the heroine. He could see through her. For example, Caroline was "trying to read [James's] mind, but then had she ever managed to read his mind? . . . [James] had always been too quick for her, reading her thoughts before she knew them herself" (Lamb, *dark dominion*: 106).

Frequently, the hero's dominance and sophistication were conveyed by difference in dress. One example showed just how far one author would go to undermine her heroine. In Rachel Lindsay's *love and no marriage*, the heroine was a renowned clothes designer (modelled after Mary Quant) and the hero was a famous novelist. When they met, she appeared inelegant; he was described as the essence of "elegance" (Lindsay, 1980: 35–38).

This last brings up an important point. He was the sex object. He ogled and leered but, in these novels, he was more often and more fully described than she. Thus, these books served to a degree as counterparts to pornography directed at men readers. Don Smith analyzed "adults only" paperbacks and found that the "men were not physically described, with the exception of their genitals, while women were described 'down to the last dimple' " (Smith, 1976: 16–24).

Descriptions of the heroes were enhanced because they were seen through the heroines'—that is, the central characters'—eyes. Even in an unsexy book like Betty Neel's *Last April Fair*, the hero was lovingly described, over and over again. For example, when he was introduced: "There was a great deal of him and he was handsome too, with a patrician nose, a firm mouth and blue eyes beneath lazy lids. His hair was so fair that she wasn't sure if it was grey or not" (Neel, 1980: 53). (Their age difference was 26 to 39.) By contrast, the first description of the heroine was concerned with "her sensible brain" (13). Of particular interest, heroes frequently appeared draped in towels, as in: "His only covering a white towel fastened loosely round his hips, and Abby's shocked eyes went from the tousled dampness of his dark brownish red hair over the sleek wetness of wide brown torso to long muscled legs and bare feet" (Graham, 1978: 26).

But Harlequin heroines were discouraged from marrying sex-objects who aroused their sexual interest. In fact, the major guideline the sexier Harlequins gave their readers was that lust was a bad basis for marriage. Why then did the fragile heroines tie up with those superior but hard-to-like heroes? A clue came from the heroines' relationships with secondary men. Often, these were supposed rivals for the heroines' affections. However, all rivals, women as well as men, were supposed rather than bona fide in these older Harlequin Romances. Secondary men were usually likable but they weren't "real men." Therefore, the heroines rejected them in favor of the heroes. Of one secondary man the heroine thought,

He wasn't a man she could ever fall in love with, but at least she didn't feel nervous of him and he was very easy to get on with. . . . She didn't find herself shrinking from him as she did from other men, as she still did sometimes with [the hero] (Pargeter, 1978: 71–72).

But the hero was preferable to the "easy to get on with" man:

What did she want? she wondered wryly. A man who would be warm and loving, but otherwise not make any demands on her time and her freedom, someone who stayed conveniently in the background? She smiled cynically to herself; that sounded more like a wife than a husband! And did she really want such a luke-warm affair when Alex had opened the door to show her what passion could hold?" (Wentworth, 1979: 173–74)

Yes, a hero was the stereotypical 1950s man who could turn girls into stereotypical 1950s women.

Here was a major dilemma: the hero aroused sexual desire in the heroine, and therefore he was her best mate. But lust was a bad basis for marriage. The heroine, to solve this paradox, had to "fuse the two halves into one." That is, she had to fuse his sexy but hard-to-like side with his loving, husband-like side.

Therefore, the hero had to have an Achilles heel. That Achilles heel was the same set of characteristics which made him a real man, his hardness and his lack of warm emotion. Harlequin Romances thus reinforced concepts held by coping women who knew they were more powerful than these heroes who were caught in their own male "Catch-22."

Heroes were physically hard and frequently denied emotions other than anger and disgust. Heroines were physically soft, often fragile, and emotional. The physical differences made allowance for particularly important "pornographic" elements that will be discussed separately. But here note further, that the hardness of the heroes represented reason and control. " 'A woman's emotional angle,' " one hero twitted his prey. " 'It can be quite as valid as logic in some circumstances,' she defended hotly. 'Not being a woman, I'm unable to follow emotional logic,' " the hero assured the reader (Hilton, 1979: 49). The heroes' control extended to their emotions and to the avoidance of all emotional entanglements with women.

The heroines represented warm emotion, and warm emotion (falling in love) overcame cold reason, sophistication, size, wealth, sardonicness, and split personality. When the heroes cracked and fell in love, softness engulfed hardness.

THE HEROINES

Their shadows lay across the sand; his large and overpowering, her own so small that she had an image of a defenseless

cave woman being dragged along by a massive, broad-shoul-
dered man with hair hanging down to his waist (Lindsay,
love and no marriage, 1980: 71).

She had forgotten the pool beside her. . . . she found herself
treading air (Mather, *images of love*, 1980: 44).

Heroines were as different as possible from heroes. Specifically,
Elizabeth Ashton stated the difference between the ideal male and
the ideal female skater, but these differences were also characteristic of other non-skating protagonists: "The man should be taller,
heavier and of course stronger than the girl. . . . Many experts
consider he should also be the more experienced of the two so
that he can adapt his speed, depth of edge and general movement
to suit the girl" (Ashton, 1979: 62). (Here, note the possibly un-
intentional sexual connotations.) But the sexes, while different,
complemented each other, especially in their sexuality. "The long-
delayed arousal of her woman's instinct [will] complement the male's
driving desire" (Graham, 1978: 47). As the relationship was com-
plementary, equality was unnecessary:

"I doubt if you'll ever learn . . . that there can never be real equality
between a man and a woman in the way you mean. There are always
times when one gives more than the other, but it evens itself out in time"
(90).

And sure enough, "in the end it evened out to a harmonious whole"
(136).

How did Oriel Millstock, Kate Darwood, Iris Ardath, and the
others manage in this inequitable situation? Unlike their men, the
strangeness of these heroines was not overtly associated with power
and dominance. Actually, these heroines were extremely powerful,
which was how they overcame their brutish heroes, and, it is es-
sential to add, probably why they were interesting to women readers. Harlequin Romance heroines from 1978 to 1982 clearly reinforced women's traditional roles. After all, if these girls could do
what they did under these circumstances, women certainly didn't
need equality. Equality would make women even more power-

ful—read, too powerful—in the view of some traditional women; or it would make them less powerful as they tumbled down to men's level, according to others (Frenier, 1984).

The heroine had one supreme power: her sexual attraction. But sexual attraction also meant danger. Furthermore, this power and danger had been enhanced by a recent sexual revolution that produced authors who wrote about Harlequin Romance heroines who realized that they were sexual beings as they pulsated after their heroes. These new heroines lusted as much as women in the Victorian male-oriented *The Pearl*, a longtime bestselling "Journal of Facetiae and Voluptuous Reading." But the heroines of sexy Harlequin Romances and Presents panted with this difference: they could lust for only one man. Even if they were widows or married (one heroine was married to a philanderer in Charlotte Lamb's *a frozen fire*, 1980), once they met the hero they realized they had never really lusted for any other man.

While portrayed as powerless, usually small, often "fine-boned" and "slim-hipped," young, naive, frequently inelegant, childlike, often unaware of their attractiveness—and while trembling, blushing, and tripping their way through the story—these lusting girls caused their heroes to lust, forced their heroes to love, inflicted pain upon their heroes, and won their heroes' hand in marriage. In fact, in these novels sexually attractive girls were so powerful that they had to be controlled by extremely dominant men and have their power undercut by all possible means.

First, a look at the two tamer novels. Their heroines lacked status, were childlike, and so forth, but did not openly lust. Yet even they inflicted pain on their heroes. Initially, they made their heroes jealous, even though this wasn't deliberate. Then, although these heroines had to come to acknowledge their love for the heroes, it was perfectly obvious to the reader that the heroes were caused to love and feel pain for some time before the heroines admitted their love (Burchell, 1980 and Neels, 1980).

The tamer heroines were not nearly as dangerous and pain-causing as those in the sexier novels. Those "girls" were almost lethal, as they combined a pure, seemingly powerless, usually virginal exterior with panting, surging, sexual desire. Of this genre, perhaps the most astonishing heroine was Winspear's Iris Ardath.

Eighteen-year-old Iris, a temporary governess, wore no make-up, and had skirts that were too long and hair that wasn't stylish. All this, because she was an orphan who had spent all her life in a Catholic convent (Winspear, 1980: 5). Her lack of experience with men was stressed (83). Not only was Iris convent-raised, but being a bastard she was cautious of men (13).

And who was this virgin of virgins to conquer? Zonar Mavrakis, the Greek tycoon. Iris's life was complicated by her reaction to Zonar. Remembering her first meeting with him, "Her skin grew warm as she tried to suppress the image [of him]. . . . [I]n her entire life she had never met anyone who made her have such thoughts and she had an urge to cross herself" (9).

Iris, like the other heroines, had to exercise huge amounts of self-control as she faced her sexy hero knowing, as did most heroines, that only a virgin could catch a hero for her groom. Of the 22 sexy novels examined, four of their heroines were not virgins. Nevertheless, these non-virginal heroines also insisted that love and acknowledgement of it should proceed sexual intercourse. An additional three heroines were virgin brides living in forced marriages (Ashton, *Reluctant Partnership*, 1979, Hilton, *snow bride*, 1979, and Whittal, *Bitter Enchantment*, 1979). These three could not consummate their marriages until their husbands acknowledged love for them. Thus, these heroines served as models of self-restraint, lusting after their husbands until love was acknowledged.

Why virginity, or at least ever more modern versions of virginity? Virginity was associated with girlhood and lack of sophistication, and women—that is, non-virgins—were scary to men: "It isn't the girls who worry me—I can deal with them. It's the older women who are far more difficult to shake off." (This was announced by the anti-marriage hero of Lindsay's *love and no marriage*, 1980: 78).

Besides, once a man had had sexual intercourse with a girl, he might lose interest because a woman of easy virtue was of little value. In *savage interlude*, the hero discussed virginity as follows: "Why pay the price of a wedding ring for something that everyone else seems to be getting for nothing?" Which suggests another aspect of virginity (Mortimer, 1979: 92).

In this modern—and awful—world, virgin women were rare, and getting rarer even in Harlequin Romances, and that made them special. "Twenty-year-old virgins went out with hula hoops," one hero averred (Dailey, *heart of stone*, 1980: 81). Virginity therefore had a manipulative value. The heroine of *A Man Called Cameron* thought about the as yet unmet Cameron:

A man with, no doubt, all a man's contemptible weaknesses. If the worst did happen she would sell the one commodity she had to sell dearly, rather than that [*sic*] part with it for nothing to one of the detestable rogues it seemed her everlasting misfortune to meet! (Pargeter, 1978: 10)

Whereas in the milder of the sexy books a kiss could make a girl a woman (76), in the sexier novels womanhood resulted from sexual intercourse. In fact, in one case womanhood was only achieved during orgasm (Mortimer, 1979: 181). That is, virginal females weren't really women.

Further, once a girl had experienced sexual intercourse and become a woman, she should be addicted to one man. The hero of *love and no marriage* said, "If I'd let you seduce me when I was ill, and we had made love, you wouldn't find it so easy to turn me down now" (Lindsay, 1980: 171). This last seems a telling clue. Once a girl experienced sexual intercourse, she would want it again and she would want it with her first lover. Therefore, no other man could precede the one true, real man, if the real man were to have sole possession. Sexual intercourse, especially if it led to orgasm for the girl, meant possession of a woman by a man, and addiction to him ensured her sexual fidelity. In *snow bride*, the heroine had just experienced her first orgasm, "and now there was no barrier to the joy of uninhibited surrender of heart, spirit and body" (Hilton, 1979: 188–89).

The fidelity of the heroines was further assured because other men's advances revolted them. "[The non-hero's] hand was on her shoulder again, and the shiver she gave was not one of pleasure" (Lindsay, *love and no marriage*, 1980: 95). These lusting heroines were thus made less dangerous; they lusted only for their real man, and their initial virginity implied later fidelity. Of course, these heroines exemplified the clichés attached to the "traditional" good woman.

However, new problems faced traditional heroines. Since their object remained marriage and marriage required a virginal girl, what were heroines to do with all their lust? First, as noted above, the heroines exerted a great deal of self-restraint. The best example was Iris Ardath, but self-mastery was also important to Lissa Vayle in Margery Hilton's *snow bride*. Here the title indicated the heroine's control. About to enter a forced marriage, "In a trance of rigid self-control [Lissa] allowed them to begin the business of helping her to get ready" (Hilton, 1979: 99).

When it finally came to exercising their lust, the heroines weren't so self-regulating.

Anna knew she had never met anyone with such an animal magnetism. It didn't matter if he shook her—shouted—hated—despaired, or, like just now, made passionate love to her. As long as he did it. Did anything (Cooper 1979: 53).

What had he just done? "A tremor ran through him—a tremor that she matched as she gave a low husky cry. 'If I had more time, Anna. . . .' and putting her unceremoniously to one side, he peeled off his shirt and threw it in a tight bundle into a chair" (53). Over and over in these novels, the lusting girl reached a point at which she was ready to lose her virginity, and at that point the hero said no. He exercised self-control, and in the process restrained her lust.

All this was in spite of assurances to the reader that all men lusted mightily—e.g., the hero of *A Man Called Cameron*: "There are those of us [men] who are perhaps a shade better in some respects. . . . But given certain situations there might be little to choose among any of us" (Pargeter, 1978: 172). This was one of frequent threats made by heroes that they might rape heroines in the heat of overwhelming male lust. Rape threats constituted a fad beginning in the late 1970s, and, for example, occurred in three of the five June 1982 Harlequin Presents.

It should be emphasized that in all but three of the total sample of sexy novels, it was the hero who thwarted sexual intercourse when both he and the heroine were aroused. The hero's command of his and of her lust established that "She had his respect at least" (Mortimer, *fear of love*, 1980: 127). But it also firmly established outside control of the heroines. Lusting women and girls have been considered great sources of danger to family and society throughout western history. The nineteenth-century conquest of white middle-class American women's sexuality was supposedly accomplished when many reformers and social pundits publicly decreed that respectable women didn't lust. That solution has broken down in the twentieth century, but the Harlequin Romances continued to be oblivious to women capable of controlling their own sexuality. These romances merely shifted control to the judgment of men, at best a muddled improvement on the status of heroines in the early 1970s Harlequin Romances, who had no sexuality to be controlled.

To further aggravate their difficulties, heroines feared their own bodies, for the heroines' bodies betrayed them. "She knew that she shouldn't respond, but her body seemed to have a will of its own" (Mortimer, 1979: 52). As a result, when the hero wasn't controlling the heroine's lust, her body was beyond her control anyway. It was well that these heroines feared their own bodies, as western tradition has it that women are dangerous and their bodies are the prime source of that danger. As in popular belief, so too in the romances there were times when the danger was heightened by the clothing heroines wore (for example, Pargeter, *A Man Called Cameron*, 1978: 86). However, clothing was a minor problem compared to other elements of the heroines' power.

Heroines could cause heroic men completely to lose their cool. In *New Man at Cedar Hills*, the hero and heroine had not been getting on. Another man commented that as a result the hero was "Snapping everybody's head off down in the horse barn" (Graham, 1978: 54). Thus, the seemingly unflappable Ben could be flustered by the naive young Abby because men were made snappish by girls who attracted them.

Indeed, men's lust was women's best weapon. The heroine of *fear of love* was a particularly powerful heroine, although she was a 17-year-old student while her hero at 34 was a famous television newscaster. He said things like "You're too much for me, Alex" (Mortimer, 1980: 86), and she sensed "his weakening towards her" (114). When he feared losing Alex, his sister-in-law said of him, "I've never seen him like that before, uncertain of himself, no self-confidence" (182). While Alex knew her own power, other heroines like Anna were less self-aware. "Anna Pearson: solo violinist– trollop–hussy–*temptress*. The idea of herself equipped to tempt a man of Gareth Evans' calibre was quite ridiculous. . . ." She thought, "Maybe his practised eye . . . recognized a voluptuousness she didn't know she possessed" (Cooper, 1979: 109–10).

Periodically these romances mentioned the physical basis for the powerlessness of heroes. Tobie in *images of love* commented on her schizophrenic hero, "less than an hour before he had been trembling in her arms. Now he seemed cool and remote" (Mather, 1980: 140).

Of additional interest was the frequent reference to heroines as "spitfires." For example, one of the most pliant heroines, Sonya of Elizabeth Ashton's *Reluctant Partnership*, had been married off by her domineering father at the suggestion of her domineering hero who, as her husband, taught her to be his skating partner. An exchange between them such as, "His eyes probed into hers. . . . She began shrinking from him. . . . [T]here was something mesmeric about his intent gaze" was typical of their relationship (Ashton, 1979: 57). Yet he said at one point, "You must be taught who is master. . . . Tonight, my little spitfire" (147). It was evident that even when lusting heroines like Sonya behaved with extreme passivity, they seemed aggressive and dangerous. And a spunky heroine such as Alex in Mortimer's *fear of love*, was punished for her assertiveness; Alex was made to seem a spoiled brat who might wilfully cause her sister to miscarry.

Heroines were dangerous because they had to be; if they weren't they wouldn't be able to guide heroes into marriage. But the heroine's danger angered the hero. Furthermore, thoughts of marriage often angered him. What a dilemma. The heroine of *savage interlude* was illegitimate and therefore especially unwilling to engage in premarital sex. When she refused to engage in sexual intercourse, he said, "Am I being paid back for the mistake your father made? . . . You like to give the come-on and then say no" (Mortimer, 1979: 112–13). Plainly, everything threatening was this girl's fault even though the mature hero "claim[ed] her lips," and "use[d] his experience to inflame her" (112–13). He said later, "You've put me through hell the last few weeks, I can't eat, I can't sleep. Only work seems to dull the pain" (125).

These dangerous girls lusted and aroused lust and, in 1950s fashion, were blamed for both. However, marriage had to be for love.

LUST VERSUS LOVE

> If [Kate] had imagined love between two people at all she
> had thought of it as a coming together of two people who
> shared the same interests and gradually grew to love each
> other. . . . But this wasn't like that at all, and yet she couldn't
> think of not giving herself to Damien (Mortimer, *savage in-*
> *terlude*, 1979: 53).

What was lust? What was love? Lisa, entrapped in her forced
marriage, "tried to harden her heart. Did she want lovemaking
without love? . . . knowing that a man could walk away from a
woman he did not love . . . even though he had just possessed
her" (Hilton, 1979: 72). Lisa's marriage was based on a five-year
contract. She thought,

If only he knew just how much she needed him! Not just the helpless
physical longing . . . but the supreme joy and satisfaction that came from
knowing she was the one woman in the world he chose to give his love
to (150).

Even in marriage (especially in marriage?) lust wasn't enough.
As one heroine said, "He only asked me to marry him because he
knew he couldn't get me into bed any other way. But once I was
his wife he'd start hating me for taking away his freedom." She
knew "that what he felt for her was nothing more than physical
attraction and than [sic] when it ebbed, as physical attraction inevitably did, there would be no genuine love to sustain the relationship" (Lindsay, 1980: 175). The impermanence of lust made
it a poor base for marriage, even while it served to lure men into
marriage.

The heroine of Whittal's *Bitter Enchantment* found herself in
love with a lusting but seemingly unloving hero.

"I can't be in love with him! . . . He's sought feminine company in the
past merely to satisfy his sexual desires." . . . She had given her love to
a man who had no need of it. . . . When he was tired of her, he would
end their marriage (98).

But often the fine line between lust and love thinned to vanishing. "She had been on fire for him, wantonly begging him to take her . . . the implications distressed and frightened her. She couldn't, she couldn't, she couldn't be in love with him!" (Bauling, 1982: 131).

One of the reasons these sexier Harlequin Romances and Presents worked was that it was difficult for the heroines to differentiate between lust and fear: "Despite everything, the man intrigued her in the most disturbing way. . . . [H]e had the power to frighten and excite simultaneously" (Whittal, 1979: 40). " 'You're afraid of me, aren't you?' . . . 'Of me, or of sex in general?' 'A little of both, I think,' she admitted" (74). This fear of the hero might really be lust for him. Sex frightened newly lusting heroines, but heterosexual heroes embodied sex. Fear gave the story psychological momentum, since the heroine had to overcome her fear in order to acknowledge her lust.

Further connecting lust and love, these romances reflected an underpinning of modern American views on marriage. In the nineteenth-century, white middle-class young people threw off parental control and developed their own criteria for mate selection. Men could choose wives on the basis of their beauty and social manners in addition to concerns such as love and companionship; women could choose husbands who would carry them to social prominence and wealth. However, even these terms failed in twentieth-century popular culture, which—mirroring and shaping a more polyglot society—came to base marital choice on the seemingly more attainable real worth of each individual. Discovering real worth meant seeing through exterior sexual attraction, even while sexual attraction remained a criterion of worthiness. Given the sexual revolution of the 1960s and 1970s, this conundrum came undone. Sexual attraction seemed mere lust, and love was supposed to be something larger.

What was love, especially given the raging lust the protagonists evidenced? Obviously love was long-lasting, "For if love was deep enough and true enough a lifetime, let alone three years, was not long enough to forget [the dead loved one]" (Hilton, *snow bride*, 1979: 30). Furthermore, love could overcome lust. Marc Nathan told his wife, Kyla, "I don't look forward to a *platonic* marriage. But if it's all you can take, I'll settle for that" (Clair, 1982: 183).

But most importantly, love created jealousy, and jealousy was the truest sign of love.

She loved this man deeply and irrevocably. Her jealousy of [her supposed rival], the ease with which [the hero] could dominate her, rebellion against his indifference and her hurt pride were now all explained. She just could not let him go out of her life even though her love was not returned (Ashton, 1979: 129).

Thus jealousy was accompanied by his ability to dominate her. In addition, love showed her respect for him. But it was jealousy that was always most important.

Her admiration and respect for his knowledge and skill in the ranching field, the only one she knew—was that love? The tearing hand of jealousy that gripped her insides when [the supposed rival] was mentioned . . . —could that be love? (Graham, 1978: 79).

Two negative emotions indicated love: first, jealousy towards supposed rivals. Never were the apparent rivals really rivals, even though they were beautiful and often sophisticated. Their glaring fault was that they were obviously after the heroes. The "supposedness" existed because the hero and heroine must love each other exclusively, and the presence of other women nurtured traditional ideas about the frightening sexual power that kept women in competition for marital "spoils." The second negative emotion was the initial hatred and antagonism between the protagonists: "Did a mocking voice whisper [to the heroine] that hate was sometimes only a kiss away from love?" (Winspear, 1979: 74).

The definition of love was similar in all the novels, the tame and the sexy. Love was mutual respect; hers for his skills and his for her individuality. (All of the heroes were extremely skillful, particularly at driving their always expensive cars. More important, all the heroes were good at their occupations and made rich by them.)

For their part, heroes respected the uniqueness of the heroines. One hero must "see under all the gook on dressed-up dolls" and find the heroine unique by comparison (Graham, 1978: 88).

Further, love was meant to last. The sexy novels departed from the tame only by dwelling on the role of lust in attaining love.

Lust entered the sexier novels probably because sex sold (probably because readers were aware of the sexual revolution and wanted to explore its meaning to them) and because in a world in which boy and girl choose each other, a major criterion for choosing had become sexual attractiveness. If sexual attractiveness triggered a relationship, women needed to know what was the connection between lust and love. These romances gave answers. And as in so many other media, the sexier Harlequin Romances and Presents, by dwelling on the passage from lust to love, created excitement.

However, not only had the heroine less control of her sexuality by the early 1980s, but in addition, unfortunately, these newer romances almost all contained sexy scenes which were sado-masochistic. (They were what some feminists termed "pornographic." By the mid-1980s, the issue of pornography had split the ranks of feminists. Hence, the term has come to seem too problematical to apply to these books. Instead, the term sado-masochism will be used here.)

For an example of sado-masochism, one can cite the old-fashioned *The Pearl*, a series of "underground" thigh-whackers written for Victorian men. In this collection, scenes of sexual intercourse alternate with scenes depicting "flogging" and "birching." Pain is a major element in the latter, but even in the scenes centering on sexual intercourse, there is a lot of hurting and coercion, especially in the activity of deflowering virgins. Newer hard-core pornography directed at men dwelled even more on pain and punishment and force than had *The Pearl* (Frenier, 1974). In fact, by 1980 one might assume that Americans were so accustomed to such depictions of pain that probably most readers of Harlequin Romances and Presents glossed over it. However, subsequent changes in the category romance industry indicated differently.

SADO-MASOCHISM IN THE SEXY HARLEQUIN ROMANCES AND PRESENTS

Each Harlequin novel is a beautiful love story—inordinately interesting, intriguingly informative, excitingly entertaining—without the overtness or violence so common in many forms of entertainment today. (Advertisement from first page inside

Sara Seale's *to catch a unicorn*, 1980, originally published 1964. This book was a free gift with the purchase of Ivory Liquid, February 1981.)

It is informative to begin with a fairly representative quote from *The Pearl*:

"Ah! you dear old fellow," said Alice. . . . "I understand everything now, and you are to make me happy by making a woman of me. . . . I know it's painful, but it won't kill me, and then, ah! the heavenly bliss I know you will make me feel" (Pearl, 1968: 54).

This section then goes on to describe his "cock" and her "pussy" and their interaction.

In 1978, Dave Sanderson, former director of marketing for Harlequin Enterprises Limited, was quoted as saying: "There is no pre-marital sex in the [Harlequin Romance] plot lines" (Maryles, 1978: 375). By 1980, this was no longer true. Not only was marital sex portrayed in the sexier Harlequin Romances, even pre-marital sex was portrayed. Nevertheless, there were as yet very few scenes of sexual intercourse, and they were less prolonged and less emphasized than the "kissing scenes" that constituted the major excitement. To illustrate, a contrast between coitus and a kissing scene in one of the sexiest novels in the sample. The protagonists of Anne Mather's 1980 *images of love* were lovers before the novel began. They had parted when he refused to marry her. As the story began, they met again, and eventually—only once in the novel—engaged in sexual intercourse.

Without [the shield of clothing] they blended together, skin against skin, softness against hard muscle, fusing together. . . . There was no thought of right or wrong, just sensuous, sensual feeling, and the mindless ecstasy of surrender. . . . She was aching for him to take her, aching for his possession, and when the consummation came, they melded together in perfect harmony (Mather, 1980: 136–37).

In contrast to copulation depicted in some of the other Harlequin Romances and Presents, there is no pain here. The operative fig-

ures are of fusing, mutual surrender, and melding in perfect harmony.

The most elaborate kissing scene from the same romance:

He . . . crush[ed] her breasts beneath the weight of his body . . . the
muscles of his thighs imprisoned hers, the hardness of his legs a disturbing
reality. His hands were at her shoulders, forcing the narrow straps of her
nightgown to yield. . . . "Robert, please—" . . . but when his lips returned to bruise hers once again, she felt herself weakening (93).

Kissing scenes like this appeared in every sexy Harlequin Romance and Presents. One more example: "She got no farther than
opening her mouth, when his firm lips instantly clamped down on
hers. . . . [T]hat mouth continued its punishing onslaught, moving over the softness of her lips with a savagery that bruised"
(Mortimer, 1982: 37).

Heroes frequently induced pain and used coercive force in these
kissing scenes. And, in the majority of cases, the heroine had no
control in these situations.

These scenes also point up the sexual symbols used in the sexier
romances. Authors could not mention penis or vulva, cock or pussy.
The euphemisms were hard, thighs, tongue, and mouth. "He sought
her mouth, parting her lips and gently probing with his tongue"
(Lindsay, 1980: 126). As the kiss was a substitute for coitus, like
coitus in *The Pearl* it was often, usually in fact, a punishment men
visited upon girls. "She had wanted Ben to kiss her . . . but not
like this, as if he was punishing her with all the harsh arrogance
of his maleness" (Graham, 1978: 113).

The heroes were violent, but what of the heroines? They were
inheritors of slap-him-in-the-face-when-he's-out-of-line philoso-
phy. But, "Fast though her hand was to rise, his was even quicker,
and she let out a gasp of pain as his fingers clamped with blood-
stopping fierceness on her wrist" (49).

Not only did these romances depict force and sado-masochistic
pain, they also dealt in two other related man-woman types of
coercion-submission: rape and woman-beating. These models were
used to control the heroines and as ways to indicate what might
well happen to girls who aroused men's lust or love, perhaps sub-
liminally to those who aroused men's desire to marry. Thus, while

the heroine had to turn lust into love into marriage, they were constantly threatened that, as they accomplished their life's mission, they might incur heavy punishment. That the heroines survived, usually unraped but not unbruised, and won the goal of matrimony, testified to their survival power, their strength, the rightness of their prize, and the method by which they obtained it.

RAPE AND WOMAN-BEATING

> "One of these days you're going to push one of us too far and find yourself raped" (the hero to the heroine, Mortimer, *savage interlude*, 1979: 131).

> "A good hiding might be a good idea," [the sheik] glanced significantly at the braided whip in his hand (Winspear, *the sheik's captive*, 1979: 122).

At one level, the readers of the sexier Harlequin Romances and Presents were told that a good man (sometimes even a not-so-good man) would never rape. For example: *Bitter Enchantment*, a tale of forced marriage in which the husband when angry at his wife "thrust her unceremoniously on to the bed and pinned her down with his body." She wept; his reaction to her tears: "If there's one thing that doesn't appeal to me, it's making love to a woman who's weeping at the thought of losing her virginity" (Whittal, 1979: 124–25).

Furthermore, readers were assured that women provoked rape—and if women provoke rape, they control it. As one hero said, after raping his wife, "You provoked me to it. . . . I'm not made of stone" (Lamb, 1980: 105). He did add, "I'm not normal where you're concerned. . . . I'm afraid that one day I'll kill you" (Lamb, 1980: 112). Another example, only one of many:

As if again she had tried him too far he pulled her closer, jerking her head back, ruthlessly plundering her protesting lips. . . .

"Let me go, you beast!"

"You only incite a man with kind words like that," he mocked (Pargeter, 1978: 158).

But much more often than rape threatened, attempted, or completed, the heroine was bruised or otherwise physically hurt by the hero. The most specific examples appeared in Charlotte Lamb's *dark dominion*. In this romance, the protagonists were unhappily married. They had quarreled when she became pregnant without his consent; two days after the quarrel, she fell down stairs and miscarried. From that time, they "drifted apart" (1980: 17). This hero treated his wife in the classic fashion of battering husbands (Martin, 1981); his jealousy was irrational and he isolated her from her friends, whom he did not like. The couple had not engaged in sex for six months when he raped her. Their marriage was saved when the heroine discovered she was pregnant again and this pregnancy transformed her husband.

dark dominion was obvious, others were less so. For example, in *snow bride* the heroine "for a dreadful moment . . . thought [the hero] would strike her" (Hilton, 1979: 98). This hurt his feelings. But she only had her "dreadful moment" after, "He moved so fast. . . . He seized her arms, his fingers biting into the soft flesh like clamps." "Tears of pain forced their way into Lissa's eyes" (98).

Even in the most egalitarian of the novels, Rachel Lindsay's *love and no marriage*, "Furiously Bart took a step toward her. Samantha recoiled in fright. 'Don't worry,' he said harshly, 'I don't think much of women, but I've never hit one' " (Lindsay, 1980: 132). Again, there's, "The crop rose and fell five times, hard," as hero beat heroine (Lamb, 1978: 34). And probable bruises—"the crushing strength of his muscular arms and the bruising hardness of his mouth" (30)—occurred in virtually all of the sexier novels.

In response, the heroines reacted like battered women. In Minnesota, a battered woman "will be defined . . . as any emancipated minor or adult woman in a relationship with a man who physically abuses her to the point where she changes her behavior in order to attempt to avoid further abuse or avoid an escalation of abuse" (*Battered Women*, 1979: 1). The most obvious battered heroine was Caroline of *dark dominion*; but Caroline was not alone.

The silence between [Jason and Melanie] was deadly, and fear knotted her stomach. . . . [H]e approached her with a look in his eyes that chilled the blood in her veins. . . . "Jason, I can explain," she began, backing away from him (Whittal, 1979: 123).

Why were these heroines raped or beaten, or at least threatened with rape and with beatings? Why did women readers read about such women? Of course there were the objective truths: women are raped and beaten and threatened with both. But it seemed more likely that since these heroines survived triumphantly to win the prize—a hero for a husband—threats and actual pain could be seen as trials gladly and necessarily undergone; a twentieth-century woman's dangerous quest, like that of medieval knights slaying dragons to win the Holy Grail. Writers and publishers may have thought this at the time, but later developments proved most American readers did not agree. In any case, until the 1980s Harlequin Romances and Presents were the only category romances available, and these heroes were the worthiest prizes available to their heroines.

THE HEROINES' PRIZE: MARRIAGE

> She felt the age-old longings of woman to be the one to tame the rogue male (Mortimer, *savage interlude*, 1979: 87).

In the tame Harlequin Romances, the protagonists were sexually attracted to each other; but more important, they spent time with each other learning to communicate their love. Communicated love led inevitably to marriage. In the sexier Harlequin Romances and Presents, physical attraction was much more important than being with each other, and learning when sexual attraction was a manifestation of love was the central problem. Communication of love followed acknowledgment that lust was its manifestation; only then could love lead to marriage, the prize.

Willingness to marry often signalled that love existed. But while marriage was not necessary for heroes, and was in fact sometimes anathema to them, marriage was a vital necessity to the heroines. Why?

Marriage meant that the heroine would not face loneliness. "[Sonya] was free, but she was utterly alone" (Ashton, 1979: 159). Secondly, marriage was equated with home and family. Heroines' "homes" were silent, lonely, and empty. Heroes' homes were filled with family and pets.

More basically, marriage was the only way heroines could be assured of permanent relationships with heroes. As the American divorce rate climbed, these romances handed out guidelines on how to get and keep heroes who didn't divorce heroines. These romances assuaged concerns about seemingly newly uncommitted husbands. They implied that heroic husbands would behave in traditional fashion in response to traditional heroines.

The price of reassurance was the heroine's fidelity but it was a small price to pay because fidelity would be mutual and would guarantee mutual possession. As the hero of *love and no marriage* insisted, "Marriage is a form of willing slavery" (Lindsay, 1980: 173).

How did the heroine—always the focal point of the novel, and usually the protagonist who had to transform the stranger into a loving spouse—unite the halves of her hero in order to enslave and be enslaved?

THE HEROINES' M.O.

> And then he laughed, a full masculine laugh that completely transformed his features, giving him a younger, carefree look. . . . "If you laugh too often people might begin to think you were almost human" (Heroine to hero, Wentworth, *Liberated Lady*, 1979: 52).

> His mouth hardened. . . . Her face flushed. . . . He smiled then, brilliantly, his eyes a vibrant blue, the strong lines of his face filled with charm (Lamb, *a frozen fire*, 1980: 70).

Fortunately (and unfortunately) for the heroines, the heroes were schizophrenic. While they appeared to be sardonic, while they threatened rapes and beatings, while they seemed cold and rational, they were also susceptible to sexual attraction and showed warmth in their love of animals and people other than the heroines. Furthermore, they were gentle when ministering to the heroines who tripped a lot and therefore needed to be ministered to a lot. Usually, readers first knew this warm side of the hero because when he smiled he was transformed. But readers were especially reassured when heroes assisted heroines. "His fingers were incredibly gentle when he pulled back the cuff on her slacks and eased off her shoe, revealing a purplish swelling under a torn stocking" (Graham, 1978: 70).

All heroes exhibited schizophrenia, but one hero specifically manifested his split personality. In *love and no marriage*, Jackson Bart (a pseudonymous author) was in real life Bartholomew Jackson (Lindsay, 1980).

As the heroine sought to understand this confusing man and to transform him into a loving husband, he frequently compounded her problem by shying away from marriage because marriage meant a loss of his freedom. "Until recently, I'd never met a woman I would be prepared to give up my freedom for" (Mather, 1982: 47). Allied with their desire for freedom, several heroes expressed distrust of women: "All women lie" (Mortimer, 1980: 111).

To overcome the hero's reluctance to marry, or his reluctance to love, the heroine capitalized on his split personality. Overcoming the hero by causing his transformation is a theme basic to much of women's fiction in western civilization. It was a constant in late 1970s best-sellers and all Barbara Cartland romances (Frenier, 1987). And as Evelyne Sullerot wrote of British, American, and French contemporary gothics: "The heroine inevitably metamorphoses the most hardhearted, the most 'brutish,' the most Caliban-like of male characters. . . . It is this character whom she will marry once she has transformed him" (Sullerot, 1979: 7n).

In these Harlequin Romances and Presents, this transformation was unconscious. Usually, as the heroine's largely unwitting sexual attractiveness combined with her conscious reluctance to engage in premarital coitus, the soft side of the hero's personality, his warm emotions, emerged. Since such emotions were associated with love, this emergence signalled to her that he was in love and, reluctantly or not, he eventually popped the question.

Most often, the precipitant was the hero's jealousy. As noted above, this jealousy was irrational and without basis. In addition, heroines felt "stabs" of jealousy as soon as they saw the heroes with other women, thought about the heroes' dead or ex-wives, or even heard them talk with other women on the phone.

Jealousy in these romances served as a signal tht the heroines, and more importantly the heroes, felt—had warm emotions. Jealousy transformed them: "The ice of his manner cracked, revealing the barbaric jealousy beneath" (Lamb, 1980: 151). Body (emotion) overcame mind (reason), the "icy cleverness of his mind failed when his body was in control" (154). And jealousy signalled love because, like love and lust—as readers were repeatedly told—jealousy was not based on reason. With jealousy and love intermingled, these novels taught that love had to be exclusive, otherwise it would arouse fury and end by disrupting any heterosexual relationship.

When heroes were jealous—snapped at people, lost their confidence, somehow manifested lack of control—they were close to confessing to themselves and their heroines that they loved. Not only was that love different from any emotion the heroes had ever felt, it also rendered them monogamous. These experienced, sophisticated, womanizing heroes were caused to realize that there would be only one woman in their lives from that time forward.

One hero went so far as to say, "even if I could never have you, I could never touch another woman again as long as I lived" (Whittal, 1979: 179). Surely this was the perfect promise of monogamy. In an especially fascinating way, two of Mortimer's heroines were further assured of their heroes' monogamy when they became impotent with other women. For example, Damien Savage, who had tried to forget Kate in the arms of other women, admitted to her,

"I'm trying to tell you—I can't take them! Nothing happens. Can you believe that?" . . .

"With your reputation—no," she said firmly.

"It's never happened to me before. I don't understand it myself" (Mortimer, 1979: 128).

Loving and monogamous, the man was won, and marriage would either soon occur or the couple would become happy. The hero would make a good husband and father. The heroines were victorious: "to know that this sometimes formidable and self-pos-sessed man needed her, was almost too incredibly wonderful to take in all at once" (Whittal, 1979: 180–81).

The heroine was now complete. Now she was assured of sanc-tioned sex, monetary security, and a permanent relationship. And the heroes were completed too. They had become "emotional," loving, caring, nurturing, and protective.

As a bonus, at the romance's end, the protagonists were com-municating with each other. No more misunderstandings, those were all cleared away. Best of all, the heroes could express their feelings for their heroines.

The heroine won a changed man:

I wanted you from the moment I met you. I fooled myself into believing we could have an affair—a long affair—even later I thought our marriage could survive my life-style. . . . Then that night when I made a jealous idiot of myself over that neighbor of yours . . . I knew that constant separations would ultimately kill what we had (Dailey, 1980: 189).

This revamped hero could divest himself of many of his far-flung business enterprises and give up champagne, hotel suites, and chateaubriand.

It is instructive to examine the heroines' *modus operandi* from the heroes' point of view. As one hero said to his heroine, "Like most females you have your own means of ensnaring a man" (Par-geter, 1978: 175). Another, "You've used my desire for you to blackmail me into marriage" (Mortimer, 1979: 167).

DANGEROUS WOMEN

"You're pushing me over the edge again" (Dominic Tempest in Mortimer, *fear of love*, 1980: 149).

The contention here is that these romances offered guidelines for behavior as well as fantasy and myth. Heroines (readers) could get their men using virginal sensual attractiveness combined with sexual fidelity. And the men (husbands) they got would become loving, communicative, sexually faithful homebodies.

A heroine who could turn a sardonic man into a perfect husband was a powerful force. And while readers were given repeated evidence that the heroines were not directly powerful, they had overwhelming evidence that heroines could be, indirectly, very powerful indeed. Moreover, for Harlequin heroines, direct power was forbidden (see for example, Wentworth, 1979).

It was indirect power that counted. This was best illustrated by the seemingly least powerful heroine, the soon-to-be-nun Iris Ardath. The hero said to her at one point,

"What makes you think you're so saintly? Women aren't called the work of the devil for nothing!"
Iris caught her breath, not so much at what he said but at the way he looked. . . . [H]e glowered from beneath his black brows, as if he wanted to reach out and shake her until her teeth rattled (Winspear, 1980: 83).

There are several elements worth noting here: (1) the most religious heroine was called the work of the devil; (2) she didn't feel insulted; (3) the hero was disturbed by her—enough to glower. In actuality, Iris was not only virginal, young, and klutzy (she did the best trip of any of the heroines when she backed off a cliff), she was also powerful. For example, she was a better parent to her charge than the boy's hero-father (44).

Iris was extremely self-disciplined as well. She not only controlled her trembling and her nerves but also her appetite (77).

In general, Iris was one of the pluckiest heroines. Zonar hated her clothes and was determined to buy her new ones. She "flashe[d],"

"And what do you intend to put me into? . . . A bikini for day and black chiffon cut down to my navel for evenings?"
"Ah [Zonar said], so the little nun has a sharp little tongue. . . . You have your nerve, young woman. How did it survive in that [convent]?"
"With difficulty—" Then she caught her breath as she realized what she had admitted to him. . . .
"So the meek little nun has a rebel hiding inside her?" (62, 93–94).

Iris was especially powerful, in that above all she was the realest of women. Zonar said that the most "intriguing women I have known were not women who painted and paraded. . . . Their warmth and reality lay in their ability to love a man beyond themselves. Could you do that?" (88). Of course she could—and did.

As the best proof of her potency, Iris won the most powerful hero in all these novels, and she won him big. Zonar Mavrakis, a self-made Greek tycoon obviously modeled on Aristotle Onassis, in the end said to Iris,

"I love you with a mad longing I haven't felt since I was a youth. . . . I could eat you. . . . I'm so hungry for you, girl. . . . Don't leave me alone to go to the devil—by the gods, if you need a good cause, then take me on. . . . There's no one but you. . . . No one since the day we met. You'll marry me?" (185–87).

Iris's victory was complete, for while she had failed as a would-be-nun, "Iris knew she had failed, . . . the radiance that was spreading inside her told her that she also won" (186). The nastiest hero of the 1982 sample, Carole Mortimer's Giles Nobles, also fell and fell just as hard. On the last page, he realized how wrong he had been about the heroine.

"Leonie, how can you still want me?" he groaned with self-loathing.
She smiled confidently at him. "It's quite simple, I can't *not* want you. Now, are you going to come back to bed with me?"
"Tonight and every other night." His words were in the form of a vow (Mortimer, 1982: 188).

THE READERS

"Harlequins help me to escape from housework into a world of romance, adventure and travel"(J. R., Glastonbury, Connecticut, quoted in Ashton, *Reluctant Partnership*, 1979: back page).

Why did married women aged 25 to 45 read these romances? Advertisements, in the front and back pages of these novels and on television, insisted that they purveyed romance and provided fantasy. "And the wonder of love is timeless. Once discovered, love remains, despite the passage of time. Harlequin brings you stories of true love, about women the world over—women like you." This ad seemed consciously to reach for that married market when it added, "Recapture the sparkle of first love . . . relive the joy of true romance" (Mortimer, 1979: 193). Furthermore, some of the Harlequin heroines read "romantic novels" for starry-eyed reasons. One found that "she wanted romantic love of the sort described in books and plays" (Ashton, 1979: 121). These novels were appealing because they were about romance and courtship, the traditional woman's most exciting adventure.

More importantly however, these books gave guidelines on how to win a prize well worth the effort: marriage to a hero. That same starry-eyed heroine gained a specific insight: "She glanced at the book with its evocative title, *The Untouched Bride*." She then suggested to her hero that their marriage be "one in name only" (134). Most importantly of all, Harlequin Romances and Presents showed wives how to get along with those unknowns, their husbands.

Harlequins gave lessons which indicated that if a woman was loving and patient and changed her behavior to suit her man, that is, if she were "traditional," he would cease to be sardonic, cruel, distant, and strange. This was a particularly important message in the five novels about forced marriage. These novels indicated that if wives behaved like battered women they would obtain and keep good marriages. However, even voluntary brides acted this way. For example, the unusually assertive Lesley Crosnier, initially considered a nymphomaniac by her acquaintances and the hero, dwindled (after encountering love) to the following thoughts: "She vowed that she would be whatever he wanted her to be: quiet when he would have her so, amusing when he was in a mood to be entertained, sensual when he had a physical need of her" (Bauling, 1982: 152).

Secondly, since all the heroines were monogamous, and since eventually the heroes either said they would be or it was implied that they would be, the reader was entertained with the importance of sexual fidelity in the midst of sexual revolution. A woman's virginity—or at second best her sexual fidelity—would guarantee a marriage that promised eternal love. Thus, for the married woman, another guideline: if she had affairs her husband would stray; if he strayed it must be because he didn't love her enough, probably because she wasn't loving and submissive enough. In either case, she was responsible for monogamy in her marriage. She could take credit for monogamy if it existed, and, if it didn't, she had the power to bring it about.

On the surface, the heroes had more power than the heroines. But underneath, the heroines had lots of unauthorized, indirect power. And that power was portrayed as being more potent than the heroes' legitimate power because it transformed brutes into husbands. In addition, the reader knew the heroines were powerful even when the heroines themselves did not. Thus the third message, especially in the sexier novels: women may appear powerless, but we really are very powerful even when we don't realize we are. Therefore, women don't need more power, and—unstated corollary—wouldn't it be unfair if we did have more power? After all, men, even heroes, had already been done in by their own lust and love for us.

But the heroine's new power was also her dilemma. In the sexy romances, she was aware that she was sexually attracted as well as sexually attractive. Lust was her lure, and it was her problem. If she had coitus with her loved one, she would lose him. Furthermore, compared to the heroines of the tame romances, sultry heroines were in a weaker position; their heroes almost always controlled the heroines' lust as well as all other aspects of their lives.

Veiled beneath anti-feminist rhetoric directed at such issues as the alleged rights of fetuses, the "breakup" of the American family, and women in military combat, lies the bedrock fear that sexuality, and especially women's sexuality, is a more dangerous threat than communism, atheistic humanism, or even out-of-the-closet homosexuality. This centuries-old bogey was compounded when the ideal nineteenth-century middle-class woman (who controlled her man's lust by having none of her own) gave way to lusting *Playboy* centerfold models who were portrayed as "girls next door." The more women's sexuality was manifested and the more it seemed to be beyond societal and patriarchal family control, the more that sexuality had to be controlled, somehow and anyhow. Therefore, the heroines of sexy Harlequin Romances and Presents were undermined in every possible way; the power of their sexuality had to be eroded.

The most obvious way to do this was to pair the heroine with a domineering hero who could control her lust. His overtly over-bearing power was appropriate because, according to traditional thought, men and women were fundamentally, irrevocably differ-ent, each had power but a different kind of power in the unsteady balance of a heterosexual relationship. This assumption led to he-roes and heroines who were so different from each other that they couldn't understand each other. And their mutual incomprehen-sion resulted in antagonism.

Possibly, this antagonism coexisted with the inability of most Americans to distinguish between pain and the ecstasy sexual in-tercourse can bring. Impressively, many twentieth-century Ameri-cans refer to physiological and psychological responses to their own sexuality as "painful." This language use combines with a Christian heritage that told us that sexual ecstasy was sinful, therefore spiritually painful as well.

Hence "punishing kisses" were supposed to be acceptable to readers of Harlequin Romances and Desires. And perhaps punish-ing kisses conveyed meaning given our lack of vocabulary. But the heroes' punishment of heroines extended far beyond kisses to steely grips which bruised, to whips that menaced and even lashed, and to threats of rape and actual rape. Thus a fourth guideline: not only did these romances hint that women readers could cope with strange husbands and create monogamous marriages—that hero-ines were really more powerful than heroes—they also indicated that the pain and damage of violence directed against women as women was an acceptable trial for heroines to undergo. However, as a study of newer products of Harlequin Enterprises Limited (which include Harlequin American Romances) and of category romances written by Americans shows, this covert guideline was less acceptable by 1984 than it was in 1977. By 1987, violence disguised as sexuality became totally unacceptable.

But since antagonism created conflict which produced the action of these Harlequin Romances, as it had in romance since Sarnuel Richardson's *Pamela*, could the genre endure without the formu-laic antagonism of strangers colliding? And what about an even more enduring covert guideline: could heroines continue to gain power over heroes by capitalizing on their gender differences in a more egalitarian story?

5

Silhouettes Aren't Harlequins: Reflections on Differences Between American and United Kingdom Authors

Harlequin Romances and Presents were so popular with American women that American publishers started 12 major rival category romance lines by 1982. The most successful began when the Pocket Books division of Simon & Schuster introduced Silhouette Romances in May 1980. Soon, this line became the most successful rival to the Harlequin Romances and Presents in the United States. Looking very much like the latter, how did Silhouette Romances differ? Did initial distinctions between these two series indicate contrasts between the effects of feminist movements in the United Kingdom and the United States?

Category romances are formulaic and written according to the guidelines of their different publishers. While staying within the romance formula (female meets male, they have problems, they solve those problems) Silhouette Romances, following their American publisher's guidelines, are not clones of Harlequin Romances. From their inception, Silhouette Romance heroes were sensitive and kind while Harlequin Romance heroes remained cruel and sardonic. Silhouette Romance love scenes were gentle and tender while Harlequin's were coercive and brutal. Last and least, in the early 1980s American heroines were somewhat feistier but less powerful than Harlequin Romance heroines.

Silhouette Romances were diligently market-researched and Silhouette Books spent millions of dollars on market research. Thus,

differences were based on more than authors' preference or publishers' whim.

SIMILARITIES BETWEEN HARLEQUIN ROMANCES
AND SILHOUETTE ROMANCES

Like Harlequin, Silhouette developed different lines: the Romance, the Special Edition, and the Desire, comparable to the
Harlequin Romance, Superromance, and Presents. (Harlequin Enterprises Limited—based in Canada—later added its Temptation
line.) Per month, Silhouette Books, like its forerunner, published
six Romances and six Special Editions, a sexier line introduced in
February 1982. This chapter will not dwell on the differences among
the three Harlequin Enterprises Limited and three Silhouette Books
lines beyond noting them.

The Silhouette Romance (about 185 pages in length), like the
Harlequin Romance, confined kissing-petting scenes to kisses and
petting with protagonists clothed. The Silhouette Special Edition
was longer, about 250 pages; the Harlequin Superromance was
longer still, about 380 pages. Both vehicles allowed for more elab-
orately plotted stories that included more frequent, longer and
steamier petting scenes in which breasts were bared and licked,
genitals touched, erections implied, and orgasms euphemistically
described. The third line of Silhouette Books, the Desire, had the
sexiest covers of any category romance line: a hot, red border
framing kissing, partially undraped couples. The Desires were the
short 185-page length of Harlequin Presents, and these seemingly
comparable lines contained sex scenes as steamy as those in the
Silhouette Special Editions and Harlequin Superromances.

In an effort to attract American readers, Harlequin American
Romances were introduced early in 1983. Attempting to cash in
on the sales of other risqué lines, Silhouette Intimate Moments
also premiered in 1983. These latter were about 250 pages long
and sizzled less than the Desire line; although Karen Solem, edi-
tor-in-chief of Silhouette Books, characterized them as "books with
the length and depth of Special Editions, the sensuality of Desire. . . . Books with the ingredient no one else has tapped: excitement" (blurb on page 2 of all 1983 Silhouette Intimate Moments).

At first glance, all these Silhouette Books seemed barely distinguishable from the lines of Harlequin Enterprises Limited. The books were the same size, the print style and page lengths were generally similar, the pictures adorning covers were almost identical, and—with the exception of the Silhouette Intimate Moments line—the names of authors of Silhouette Books dominated titles as in the Presents, the best selling Harlequin line during the early 1980s.

Given all these similarities, there existed differences that may have indicated the tastes of American women readers of category romance. They certainly did say a great deal about American writers and publishers of those romances. The first and probably most important difference: United Kingdom women wrote Harlequin Romances, Superromances, and Desires. In 1980, there was one exception, the extremely prolific and popular American author Janet Dailey. Americans, with some exceptions, wrote Silhouette Books. Acknowledging Silhouette's popularity, Harlequin Enterprises Limited added its American Romance line in 1983; this series was written by American authors.

DIFFERENCES BETWEEN SILHOUETTES AND HARLEQUINS

To study the differences, six summer 1982 Silhouette Romances, three summer 1982 Special Editions, and three 1982 Desires were used here. All but one of their authors were American. After realizing the differences between the products of Harlequin Enterprises Limited and Silhouette Books, two Janet Dailey Silhouette Romances were added to the sample. Finally, to further confirm differences between British and American authors, five Harlequin American Romances and five Second Chance at Loves, an American line published in 1982–83, were added.

Turning to the differences themselves—beyond the obvious contrasts in setting, language, grammar, and life-style—the most important dissimilarities between Silhouette Books and Harlequin products were in their heroes and love scenes, but also striking were some of the disparities in their depictions of heroines.

A word about "heroines." In no way were women protagonists female heroes in the literary sense. Carol Pearson and Katherine Pope found, "Because negative myths about women are internalized through the socialization process, the first task of the female hero is to slay the dragons within." The literary female hero then "wins the treasure—that is, the liberation of her true, vital, and powerful self" (Pearson and Pope, 1981: viii). The heroines of the Harlequin novels and Silhouette Books were merely protagonists, and only in that sense were they heroes. They did not act so much as they reacted, and the treasure they won was marriage to a hero, not self-possession.

Heroes and Their Love Scenes

The heroes of the 1977–1982 products of Harlequin Enterprises Limited were nasty and cruel; Silhouette Books heroes were much nicer. Excluding Janet Dailey's category romances, in the 17 Silhouette Books read for this chapter only three heroes were nasty. An example was Dr. Curt Pride of Jeanne Stephens's *Pride's Possession*; although he was pushy (many other heroes of Silhouette Books were too) and lacked understanding, he could be kind and sympathetic to the heroine, as when her mother became ill. (In 1977–1982 Harlequin Enterprises Limited books, the hero would have been kind to the mother while remaining unkind to the heroine.) Two of the Silhouette Books' heroes were not mean but were described as arrogant and hard-driving. Surprisingly, three of the heroes were sensitive; there were no sensitive heroes in the 1977–1982 Harlequin products. For example, the Silhouette Books' hero Rand Alastair of Stephanie James's *Corporate Affair* was twice described as vulnerable, and Jace Matthews in Nicole Monet's *Love's Silver Web* was actually described as scared, an emotion unimaginable in a Harlequin Enterprises Limited hero. Astonishingly, Jay Gattling of Möeth Allison's *Love Everlasting* apologized after their first act of sexual intercourse, "At my age [he was 42], I ought to do better. . . . forgive me if I disappoint you" (Allison, 1983: 157).

For an example of nastiness American-style, Stephens combined a hard-hitting hero lacking in understanding with a heroine who protested to the point of childishness. When she said she didn't want to talk with him,

"I think maybe you do," he told her with that maddening self assurance that had often infuriated her at work.

"Don't tell me what I want!" She moved to wriggle past him and he stepped to one side so that she found herself still faced with his long, lean body. . . . She flung her head back determinedly. . . . He caught her chin in strong fingers and kept her head thrust back. . . . His gleaming green regard focused on her mouth.

"Let me go! What do you think you're doing?"

Her hand flailed toward his mocking face and he easily caught her wrist before the hand met its target (Stephens, 1982: 63).

Much more common were scenes in which the hero behaved well enough—if the descriptive passages were ignored.

Another difference between the heroes of Harlequin products and those of Silhouette Books was that the former were nasty with little reason; when the Americans were vicious, they had a real rather than imagined reason. United Kingdom heroes, like Mortimer's Giles Noble, were ill-natured because they believed, without proof, that the heroines were promiscuous. On the other hand, Stephen's Dr. Pride was typical of American heroes. He and Sara Dantan had a legitimate disagreement at the hospital when she was an administrator and he a surgeon: should money be spent to expand surgical facilities or medical research? Another telling difference—again leaving until later Dailey's Silhouette Books—American heroes cooked food. United Kingdom heroes never did.

In fact the whole attitude toward cooking and food was different. At least two of the Silhouette Books heroines were gourmet cooks. Food both at home and in restaurants was more often described. Heroines got hungry much more often; in contrast, the heroines of the Harlequin books constantly lost their appetites. In one Silhouette Book, Fern Michaels's *Nightstar*, the heroine even binged on food. Eight of the 17 heroes definitely could cook, and one of the nine who was not described while cooking was the hero of British author Anne Hampson's *Stardust* (1982). The point is, that American heroes were performing what in Harlequin Romances and Presents had been "women's work" and, in the process, underlining their more androgynous behavior.

With these disparities in mind, a study of Janet Dailey's heroes indicated similar switches from cruel to sensitive.

The American Janet Dailey is a very special category romance author. By August 1981, she had written 65 books and, by August

1984, 100 million copies of them had sold. These books, published in 17 languages, sold in 90 countries (Berkeley, Aug. 16,
1984: 16–17). By 1981, Dailey was the fifth bestselling living novelist in the world. And in August 1987, she was only 43 (Walters,
Jan. 1982: 35–36; May 1982: 35–36). Dailey has published with
Harlequin Enterprises Limited, Silhouette Books, and as a best-
seller author with the Pocket Books and Poseidon divisions of Simon & Schuster: for example, *Touch the Wind*, 1979; *Night Way*,
1981; and *Silver Wings, Santiago Blue*, 1984. In 1986, *Silver Wings*
sold 1,335,000 copies and, along with Dailey's *The Glory Game*,
constituted 57th and 69th of 103 books selling over a million copies
in 1986 ("Mass Market Paperbacks," 1987: 28). Furthermore her
hardback *Heiress*, selling for $17.95, was 16th on *The New York
Times Book Review* bestseller fiction list on August 16, 1987.

Brock Canfield of Dailey's *heart of stone* (published November
1980) was the nastiest Harlequin Enterprises Limited hero in the
1978–1982 sample. In Dailey's Silhouette Books, Bickford Rutledge of *The Hostage Bride* and Race Cantrell of *Wildcatter's
Woman* were described as arrogant; but Rutledge knew fear, unlike most heroes of Harlequin Romances and Presents, and neither
of Dailey's Silhouette Books heroes behaved in a gratuitously mean
fashion, as did Brock Canfield. Furthermore, both Rutledge and
Cantrell showed a weakness as they "dove" for a bottle of scotch
(Dailey, 1981: 111) or arrived at the heroine's shop drunk (Dailey,
1982: 100), actions foreign to Harlequin Romance and Presents
heroes.

What is to be made of these differences? It appears that—like
men characters in American daytime soap operas (as Tanya Modleski pointed out, "Soap operas may be in the vanguard not just
of T.V. art but of all popular narrative art," Modleski, 1982: 87)—
heroes in Silhouette Books were relatively sensitive and lacking in
macho nastiness. As Rita Estrada, founder of Romance Writers of
America, said concerning American writers in June 1982, "Macho
is out" (Truehart, 1982: 24).

The implication is that American romance writers idealized men
who, although older, richer, and more sexually experienced than
their heroines, were sensitive to and understanding of them. The
love scenes in sexy Harlequin Romances and Presents and Silhouette Books elaborate this difference. Punishing kisses dominated

the former (punishing kisses were always visited by heroes upon heroines, never vice versa); and although punishing kisses appeared in Silhouette Books, they were outnumbered by gentle, sexy, senuous kisses which sometimes became possessive and demanding.

A number of 1978–1982 heroines of Harlequin books were turned on by violence. An example from Bauling's *wait for the storm*:

> He jerked her roughly against him, his mouth descending on hers in fierce assault, and Lesley didn't even have time for a gasp of surprise.
> Rad showed her no mercy. . . .
> "You're hurting me," she gasped.
> "That's all you deserve, sweetheart," he retorted. . . .
> Her lips felt swollen . . . yet even as he continued his raid on her senses without tenderness or respect, Leslie thrilled to the warmth of his body and was carried away on the dark tide of desire (Bauling, 1982: 145–46).

American heroines could react in this masochistic way, but more often when a punishing kiss was involved they were not aroused.

> He reached out and pulled her to him with bruising swiftness and savagely brought his lips down on hers. It was not so much a kiss as it was a mark of possession. . . . Then abruptly everything changed.
> As if her shock and surprise halted his suddenly emotional reaction, his savagery gave way to gentleness that devastated her (Drummond, 1982: 130).

This marked differences between Harlequin Presents and the lines of Silhouette Books underscored the disparities between their heroes and added one more. American writers, in addition to devising sensitive and understanding heroes and heroines who did not want physical punishment in lovemaking, made it clear that heroes should be pleasing at sexual foreplay.

Heroines

The heroines in Silhouette Books, like those in the products of Harlequin Enterprises Limited, varied from wimpy to feisty. There did seem to be fewer spineless heroines in this sample. However, while unwarranted nastiness was characteristic of many of the latter's heroes, but not of most heroes of the former, it was disconcerting to find it typical of some heroines of Silhouette Books.

To compare: of the heroines in the six 1982 Harlequin Presents, three were not wimpy, two were, and the sixth was stranded somewhere between gutsy and ineffectual. Carole Mortimer's heroine, the best example of timorousness, put up with the most gratuitously bad-tempered hero of the lot, and furthermore capitulated to him as her lust, which she equated with love, overcame her recognition that he was a complete boor. She surrendered most tellingly after he threatened to break her wrist and demanded "sole rights to your body and time" (Mortimer, 1982: 125). Then, when he left her, "Her mouth drooped with disappointment. 'Don't you say goodnight anymore?' " she asked. "She so much wanted him to kiss her" (126).

At the other end of the Harlequin Presents spectrum, as noted in the last chapter, was 20-year-old Lesley Crosnier of Bauling's *wait for the storm*, who, though a virgin, was perceived to be a nymphomaniac. Her conversation was extremely sophisticated, she was assertive in relationships with men, and she did not crumble when her father was discovered to be a thief. However, like many of the feistier heroines of Harlequin Presents, she appeared spoiled because she was assertive and strong-willed. This was the price feisty Harlequin Presents heroines usually paid.

Of the Silhouette Books heroines, five were wimpy or fairly wimpy, six were spunky or fairly spunky, two added gratuitous nastiness to their spunk, five were in-between, and one marvelous heroine was cheerfully easygoing. Unlike the other uptight heroines, this last was not defensive and did not take personally every remark her hero made (Browning, 1982).

While the Silhouette Books heroines were only a little less impotent than their Harlequin counterparts, some of them gave the impression of assertiveness when they either directly initiated sexual action or actually asked for completion of sexual intercourse. Neither of these initiatives ever occurred in the sexy Harlequin Presents. But in four cases among the Silhouette Books—one, the spineless heroine of English author Hampson's *Stardust*—heroines initiated sexual action by kissing the hero or asking that sexual action begin. In four Silhouette Books, all either Special Editions or Desires, heroines during sexual foreplay said: "make love to me, Hoyt" (Baker, 1982: 14), "Make love to me, Court" (Stephens, 1982: 205), or a similar variant.

The heroines thus gave the impression that they were directly desirous of sexual intercourse and able to demonstrate or voice that desire rather than wait, panting, for the hero to act, as in the Harlequin Presents. American heroines here evinced an aspect of the sexual revolution; women should have some control over heterosexual intercourse.

Somewhat sexually assertive, American heroines nevertheless exhibitied ambivalence when it came to exercising power over the balance of their professional and personal lives. Their power and autonomy can be judged on two bases: the way in which heroines fared as career women, and the extent to which they had control over their personal decisions to marry, remarry, or make their marriages long-lasting.

Of the 1982 Harlequin Presents heroines, three had no jobs at the beginning or end of the novels, but three would continue in their careers. On the personal level, five mutually agreed to marry, without contingency concessions on either hero or heroine's part. In one, however, the hero conceded to give up one job in order to take another which would not keep him from home (marriage) for long period of time (Bauling, 1982).

Of the 17 heroines of the Silhouette Books, three had no jobs, seven kept their jobs (two of these were sexier Desire heroines), two probably would keep their jobs, but three gave them up. Four of the five heroines of the 1983 Silhouette Intimate Moments kept their jobs. In other words, most of these heroines did not give up their jobs or careers to marry. Two men made career concessions to marriage, one gave up a corporate career to run a winery (Drummond, 1982), and another would probably operate his corporate offices from the west rather than the east coast in order to be close to his heroine (Allison, 1983). In the most ambivalent example, the heroine was ready to give up her career, but her hero made her his business partner (Goforth, 1982).

In the personal area, the pattern was like that of the Harlequin books. Fourteen Silhouette Books couples married mutually without concession or coercion on either part, and one hero made a personal concession—he would marry for love rather than family approval (Hope, 1982). But perhaps of greatest interest, in two Silhouette Books the heroes picked up their gutsy heroines, threw them over their shoulders, and marched them off to marriage, John Wayne–style (Browning, 1982 and Roberts, 1982). This proved to be a very temporary fad; the five newest Silhouette Books cited here did not contain such scenes.

Conclusion

To many American women, Silhouette Books must have come as welcome respite from the products of Harlequin Enterprises Limited. For example, Janice Radway's readers would have found them more satisfying. Frequently, the American heroes were responsive toward and insightful about their heroines, and heroes of Silhouette Books were more androgynous than the United Kingdom heroes. This is not to vindicate concepts of androgyny. As Showalter noted, "Whatever else one may say of androgyny, it represents an escape from the confrontation with femaleness or maleness" (Showalter, 1977: 289). Silhouette Books, like Harlequin Enterprises Limited romances, escaped from all such confrontations. Nevertheless, unlike the latter, Silhouette Books did portray heroes engaged in women's work as well as heroines engaged in men's.

In addition, all of the heroes of Silhouette Books were less likely to punish their heroines physically. It must be noted that, in the sexier Silhouette lines, a brutal grip sometimes replaced punishing kisses; however, since the general tone of these lines was less violent and more erotic, Silhouette Books put physical pain further outside direct sexual interaction than did Harlequin romances. In Ann Barr Snitow's and Ann Douglas's terms, they were even softer porn.

As Carol Thurston and Barbara Doscher noted about best-seller heroines, early 1980s category romance heroines were often career oriented and frequently engaged in sexual intercourse before marriage. In these as in other areas, the authors of categories copied innovations pioneered by authors of romantic best-sellers. In the more recent 1983 Silhouette Books, heroines all remained on the job after their relationships with the heroes were consolidated. Even the least assertive heroine probably continued to head her school for sight-impaired girls (Bird, 1983). Still, category heroines were primarily sexually faithful to heroes who were monogamous, which perhaps satisfied the readers Radway studied.

Another trend in American category romances was the older heroine. The average age of the heroines in the Silhouette Intimate Moments was 29 1/2, and in two cases the heroine and hero were closer in age than was usual in Harlequin Romances and Presents. The average age of the heroine in The Second Chance at Love series was 25 1/2; and of five Second Chance couples, two were the same age. Finally, in the Harlequin American Romances, the heroine's average age was 26 and the average difference in age was six years, significantly less than the average age difference in Harlequin Romances and Presents.

Other differences and similarities were also illuminated by reading the American-line Second Chance at Love, and especially by reading five 1983 Harlequin American Romances. One of these latter epitomized American themes examined here. Rebecca Flanders's *Twice in a Lifetime* presented the nicest, most sensitive hero in all the category romances cited in this chapter. Kyle Waters was insecure, apologized for his boorish behavior (Flanders, 1983: 33), and even lost his balance (47). (In the lines of Harlequin Enterprises Limited, heroines continued to trip and sprain ankles, but heroes never, never did.) Furthermore, Kyle waited patiently for widow Barbara Ellis to get over her first marriage and even gave up his architecture for painting in order to spend time with his new wife and his children by his first marriage. Last, he never kissed punishingly nor did he brutally grip the heroine. Nevertheless—an example of the ambivalence in American category romances concerning changes in women's lives—although Barbara was on her way to a successful editing career, she dropped said career without even bothering to notify her boss and flew from Maine to be with Kyle in Oregon and raise his two-year-old twins.

One more important difference: unlike the other heroes of Harlequin products, the tender heroes of American category romances were not hostile to women. Therefore, they were more likable and their American heroines were not forced to see cruelty as love. Moreover, along with this psychological shift came a resultant development in Silhouette Intimate Moments: this series was meant to and often did include more of the hero's point of view than had other category romances, a trend that was in direct response to readers' suggestions.

Tania Modleski had important things to say about the probable result of such a trend. She noted that the third person viewpoint of 1970s category romances allowed readers to view the heroines' story-fantasy as their own, when heroines were not more objectively described. In the process, the reader was torn between playing the observer and becoming the observed heroine (Modleski, 1982: 55–56). This reinforced the reality that an American woman is taught to observe herself as men see her. As Modelski added, "What Harlequins are read for is the way they deal with the contradiction between the ideal situation and real life, in which women are presumed guilty (. . . of scheming to get a husband) until proven otherwise" (52).

Modleski pointed out that the reader might disappear from reality into a category romance where the heroine was not scheming to get a mate, but then re-emerge into reality and feel scheming, therefore acknowledging an artificially (romance-) induced guilt (56). Only insofar as the reader of a romance knew what the heroine knew could she assume that the hero would be stricken by love and that the end would be happy. The reader's capacity for distancing herself from the heroine was further enhanced in Silhouette Intimate Moments when she read that the hero acknowledged being stricken by love and described the effects of the love he was experiencing.

In spite of all these changes, American category romance heroines were only slightly less reactive and little more active than their United Kingdom predecessors and 1982–1983 counterparts. American heroines continued to seek the marital prize to the exclusion of significant personal growth.

In summation, the differences between the products of Harlequin Enterprises Limited and Silhouette Books indicated that American authors had incorporated the feminist stress on changing men's gender roles, but that the British may have better understood the need for women's economic and personal autonomy. Unfortunately, United Kingdom authors still extolled brute heroes, and American romances continued to encourage a fantasy life based on the desire to abdicate responsibility for a liberation of a powerful self (see Dowling, 1982). On both sides of the Atlantic, readers continued to be encouraged to escape into a fantasy that could, according to Modleski, induce guilt upon their re-emergence into reality.

6

Under American Influence: Category Romances in the 1980s

After the introduction and ascendancy of American authors, the most popular category romances incorporated their use of the recent women's movement and sexual revolution in the United States. These authors dominated because of a new sophistication on the part of category romance readers.

By 1982, it was clear that many readers of category romances bought books written by their favorite authors, ignoring whether they bore the imprint of a specific romance line. In order to compete, many publishers tried to resurrect brand loyalty by developing products similar to romances by those authors.

ROMANCE PUBLISHERS FIGHT IT OUT

From their introduction until 1982, Harlequin Presents had constituted the most consistent romance line. Within its girl-met-man plot, a reader could always count on brutal heroes and stumbly heroines. But now Harlequin Presents had serious rivals, and victim heroines and sardonic heroes no longer sold well. First influenced by best-seller romances and then by American category romances, Harlequin Enterprises Limited experimented as it tried to find a salable new formula.

By 1982, the single bestselling category romance line was Silhouette Desires; its authors set the new pattern for Harlequin Enterprises Limited as well as other lines. Yet the Desires were amazingly inconsistent in a number of areas, particularly in depictions of the heroine's character. Catching up to the new market, Silhouette Books realized that readers wanted to read about sexual action and cared less about other formulaic devices. Readers who chose the Desires bought them for their frequent, lengthy, and newly explicit sex scenes.

Also trying for the newer market, Second Chance at Love, the most interesting American line, presented its sexuality in a new format involving older, therefore more sensually aware, heroines. In fact, the guideline sheet sent by its publishers to hopeful authors was very specific about this.

Mild lovemaking should be introduced as early in the story as is convincingly possible and should gradually build in intensity until the couple actually makes love, by about half-way through the story. They should make love at least once more in the second half of the book. Actual lovemaking should be described in considerable length—in several pages rather than in several paragraphs—and with plenty of sensual detail (*Second Chance*, 1982: 4).

Perhaps the most predictable romance line in 1982, Second Chance at Love appealed to women's angers and frustrations in their own marriages, and pointed to certain realities in women's lives. For if in 1970 it had been difficult for average romance readers—married, middle class—to identify with a young, virginal, tripping, working-class heroine, by the 1980s it was harder for them to believe that the heroine would never love anyone but the first man with whom she had sex. Most married readers had experienced pre-marital sex themselves (Tavris and Offir, 1977) and had at least thought about divorce (Bernard, 1973). Publishers became willing to trade on the regret that eternal, obsessive ecstasy—the kind of love sold by most of American popular media most of the time—had somehow passed many readers by. Second Chance at Love explicitly played on this particular reader fantasy. As the back cover of every one stated,

The heart
doesn't count the years—or the tears. And if
romance is grand the first time,

there is nothing more precious than your
Second Chance at Love

Of course, before one could have a second chance at love, something had to happen to Chance #1. The guidelines spelled it out:

Her first relationship must have been serious enough for her to have felt
she was in love and committed, and it must have ended before the start
of the novel. The heroine can be a divorcée, a widow, or perhaps jilted
for a reason that does not reflect badly on her (*Second Chance*, 1982: 2).

Either Chance #1 was a wimp or a rat and the break up was not
her fault; or Chance #1 was also the Second Chance at Love, in
which case the misunderstanding that had split them apart was
usually her fault. In either case, she had desperately wanted to
make her first relationship work. When that relationship failed,
Second Chances indicated that with Mr. Second Chance at Love
the heroine could finally find her eternal, exciting, obsessive, true
love. Married women could fantasize that their husbands might
reform, or be reformed, into second chances, or, more revolution-
ary, that husbands could be replaced by second chances.

Searching for readers in a seemingly brand new market, Candlelight Ecstasy and Ecstasy Supreme presented perhaps the least consistent products of all. They ranged from romances containing brutal
heroes to ones containing the most sensitive, feminist heroes to be
found in any romance line in the early 1980s. Furthermore, they
frequently included more character and plot development than any
other line outside the To Have and To Hold series. Daringly, Can-
dlelights contained plot elements that were specifically forbidden
in guidelines for other romance series, such as espionage themes
and gothic devices, although certainly these elements were always
secondary to the primary motive—the love story. Some Candle-
lights even flirted with an element never found in any other romance line except the short-lived Finding Mr. Right: a secondary
man with whom the heroine was sexually involved. In all the other
category lines, this kind of relationship had to be over before the
story began.

In summation, while Second Chances were the most explicit, all
these lines included previous sexual experience. This was one of

the most signficant differences between early 1980s American category romances and the old formula. Since the new heroine had
experienced lust toward someone other than the hero, to some
extent the hero's power over her was reduced. The hero no longer
owned her entire sexual history. This new heroine defied the traditional belief that men needed virginal wives because such wives
could be sexually controlled. And the new heroes did not object
to non-virgin heroines (although in those romances in which the
heroine was virgin, the hero was always very pleased). Furthermore, these newer romances disavowed the basic theme of late
1970s category romances, that lust equals love. They attempted to
get around that equation by having the heroine lust more after the
hero than she had ever lusted before. In any event, the new heroine was allowed experience previously granted only to heroes: lust
unrelated to True Love.

The non-virginal heroine was the key to the most important
new plot device. The hero and heroine could now leap into bed at
their first or second meeting, circumventing any virginal reluctance
and allowing the novel to contain more and steamier sexual scenes.
Authors became adept at circumventing the traditional implications of the heroine's non-virginity, and at turning experience into
a new mode of innocence:

> At long last she slid to his side, still clinging to him, dizzy with happi-
> ness.
> "I never expected anything like this to happen to me," he said softly.
> "Neither did I."
> "I think this is the first time I've really been in love."
> "I feel the same way," she whispered, touching his lips with her finger-
> tips.
> "I wish we'd met years ago," he said. "I would've liked to be your first
> and only lover."
> "I feel as if you are. Waiting so long for someone like you only makes
> it more wonderful. But if we'd met years ago, maybe we wouldn't have
> been ready for each other."
> "Sometimes you're too smart for your own good," he said drawing her
> against his chest (Andrews, 1984: 132).

There were a number of other ways in which the various American romance lines continued to differ from the older Harlequin

Romances and Presents. The heroes weren't ruthless. They were opinionated but they were also boyish, playful, and generally much more easygoing. While earlier heroes were somewhat like Aristotle Onassis, American romance heroes seemed more like Tom Selleck. The American hero did not behave coldly to the heroine, nor did he dislike her from the beginning of the romance. He did not deny emotion, he seldom threatened rape or punishment, he didn't emphasize the heroine's difference from other women, he was seldom ultra-rich or ultra-famous, he did not think love was a myth, nor did he wish to fight it off. He did not treat the heroine like an immature child, nor did he have to rescue her all the time. Again, he was not very much older than the heroine; in fact, he was often the same age, and could even be younger.

The heroines of American romances also continued to differ markedly from the 1977–1982 Harlequin Romance and Presents heroines. Not only was the American heroine usually not a virgin; she was older, had a professional career, didn't stumble around the hero, didn't dislike him on meeting him, wasn't insecure about his love, and didn't always lose arguments with him. She had friends of the same age and social rank, and often her supposed rivals were nice women rather than nasty manipulators. And heroines behaved casually around heroes, even joking with them on occasion; no humor had been allowed in the older formula. Thus, the heroes and heroines of American romances were more believable, less schizophrenic, and more likable.

Nevertheless, there were many ways in which the early 1980s American romances mirrored late 1970s vintage Harlequin Romances and Presents. The notably larger hero was his own master and usually the most powerful man in the context of the story. He manifested jealousy, which signified love to the knowing reader. He was the story's primary sex object and incited lust in every woman who ever met him; and, like the earlier hero, he was ruled by his loins.

As in the Harlequin Romances and Presents, the American heroine lusted, had no effective family, was nervous around the hero, and totally sexually satisfied only by him. She continued to exercise some manipulative power over and by means of the hero, although, as before, she loved him because he was wonderful, not because he was powerful.

Like earlier ones, American romances remained opposed to promiscuity and infidelity. Usually, love and lust, while less often equated, remained equally important to marriage. In fact, comparisons of the various romance lines make it obvious that their most important elements were sex and obsessive love, and that these were still the basic elements of the heroines' power.

In many ways traditional power was being undermined, however. "Traditional" readers were being faced with new power fantasies. If the heroine's most important form of power was manipulation, then by decreasing the hero's measure of direct power and developing the heroine's—by making the protagonists more equal in status, age, intelligence and sexual experience—the need for and the strength of women's manipulative power was diminished. Therefore, any attraction readers felt for portrayals of female manipulative power was discouraged.

American lines seemed to be developing away from the love story as the exclusive motive, with manipulative power as the operative fantasy, and moving more in the direction of suspense-romance writers like Victoria Holt, Mary Stewart, and Phyllis Whitney. In their stories, the heroine's status was as great as the hero's and the plot involved both of them in a united exercise of direct power against villainous odds.

THE ROMANCE MARKET SLUMPS

As the romance market began to dwindle in 1984, American publishers responded to readers' requests and made additional changes. The most obvious consisted of adding brief story sections told from the hero's point of view. Dwelling on the hero's emotional reactions made him seem sensitive. This device allowed readers to run ahead of both protagonists, knowing even more surely than the hero or heroine that the story would come out well in the end. Other innovations included new definitions of love and romance, and overt and covert incorporations of feminist ideals.

At first, the hero's viewpoint was posited only in romances about married couples. Of particular note in this regard was the To Have and To Hold line. This was the most realistic romance line encountered in this study, and it concentrated on a second new element as well. Since many of the protagonists were married, they had had time to reflect on love and their definitions of love. Sometimes that reflection meant little as couples continued to equate love with lust. But at other times the definitions were more intriguing. As in, "To me, the greatest immorality in the world is to clutch someone to you who doesn't love you or want to be with you," said Melanie Randolph's heroine Beth Columbine (Randolph, 1983: 130–31). And Jennifer Rose's heroine, Dena Klein, thought that love was "a blend of heady infatuation and profound friendship" (Rose, 1983: 6).

The most detailed definition was given in the best category romance of all those read for this study. Mary Haskell's Larry Andrews had married Jenny 15 years before the story began. Jenny had never been sure why he married her instead of his first love. At the end of the novel he told her,

"When I first met you, you seemed like a serious little girl. Then I began the incredible adventure of discovering all the complex facets of you. Your quick, inquisitive mind. . . . Your little bursts of humor . . . your amazing insights. Your constant, unwavering interest and faith in me. Do you know what that does for a man? I married you because I loved you. Because you made everything in my life richer and fuller, because you made me happy. That has never changed" (Haskell, 1983: 179–80).

Thus a new concept of love existed, but what of romance? Romance—largely undefined—is what romance lines are supposed to be about. But romance is seldom overtly discussed in any of the books. Dena Klein did say at one point, "And marriage without romance—" To which her husband responded, "Is like smoked salmon without dill" (Rose, 1983: 75). By 1984, romance was principally an aura: candles, lace, fine food and wine, and sensual lovemaking. In the earlier Harlequin Romances and Presents, romance had been more than an aura: it was monogamy between a traditional self-effacing heroine and her all protecting hero-husband. In the newer American lines, monogamy was not only tempered by the heroines' previous sexual experience, it involved dual-career wives with androgynized husbands. These American protagonists were contemporary people touched by the 1970s women's movement. In fact, feminism—the third new element—was frequently suggested, although less frequently discussed, in all these novels.

Feminism and feminists had been treated with scorn in the products of Harlequin Enterprises Limited throughout the early 1980s. But by 1984 in American categories, feminism was assumed. It was thoroughly discussed in Randolph's *Heart Full of Rainbows*. Homemaker Beth and realtor Joe Columbine had been married for nine years and had had three children. She wanted to return to college and finish her undergraduate education. He did not have enough money to send her back to school and didn't want to admit that. His feelings were further complicated by the fact that Beth was a much better money manager than he. She took a part-time job, financed her education, and discovered her talents while working as research-writer-assistant to a Harvard professor. Joe was upset by these changes and ruminated to himself,

Why had [Beth] let these women's libbers get to her? . . . Now you even had to fill quotas of women when hiring. And just let some mean-natured boss like Springfield dump on women the way he routinely did on men. Just let him try! Women yelled discrimination and even sexual harassment so loud the building fell down. They didn't want *equal* rights; they wanted the deck stacked neatly in their favor (Randolph, 1982: 15).

Feminism was overtly mentioned in other To Have and To Holds. For example, one hero said, "Now I've let myself in for one of your women's lib lectures" (Connolly, 1983: 9). And there were put-downs of feminism. For example, Rose's heroine, Dena, wanted a baby, but

She wasn't going to be a mother in the mold of some women she knew, insisting that their husbands share the chores fifty-fifty. . . . Yet Richard would probably, of his own volition, end up doing more for her and the baby than those other women's husbands. Not out of guilt, not because he would feel he had to prove he was a liberated male, but because he loved Dena and would love the baby and was a very good man (Rose, 1983: 155).

This of course meant that the traditional woman could have more than the modern woman if she had the right husband. Which moved into an even more interesting area, descriptive of the ways in which these heroines actually behaved and thought in general, rather than what they said or thought about feminism.

Four of the five heroines of the 1983 To Have and To Holds sometimes thought and behaved in feminist ways. The most feminist heroine was Beth Columbine; but other heroines, like Robin James's Christine, thought about "the trust fund of hers that [her husband] tried so hard not to have any Old World male hang-ups about" (James, 1983: 70). Even Rose's heroine, Dena—whose husband needn't prove he was a liberated male—at one point said to her husband: "Did I forget to read the fine print in our marriage contract? Did it say that you were allowed to have another job besides *us*, but I was supposed to be Mrs. Klein, period and end of sentence?" (Rose, 1982: 143).

In light of such discussions of feminism and feminist thoughts and behaviors, did these heroines give more than they got in order to maintain their marriages? Beth would continue to study and write at the end of *Heart Full of Rainbows* and Joe, speaking midst his large Italian-American family, concluded, "No . . . I'm not the bosso. I'm the husband. Beth's the wife. . . . Two parts of a whole. Equal" (Randolph, 1983: 180). Connolly's protagonists were from two different worlds—Irish theater and Hollywood movies and television. In the end, Katie would perform in Irish plays and Hollywood movies; Brian, in Irish plays and on Hollywood television. In the context of the story, Brian, like Joe, gave more than his wife to the relationship. Only Rose's Canadian heroine retreated from her career goal, to be owner-chef of a Kosher restaurant. The restaurant took up too much time, just as her husband had insisted it would. But while she retired to have a baby, she also would write a cookbook. The last two pages of the romance contain Dena's recipe for Pâté Royal (Rose, 1983: 179–80).

A look at April 1984 Harlequin Presents may be elicited to test the scope of these changes. Their heroines' average age was 24; the heroes', 32; the average age difference was 8 years. Thus these heroines were older and closer to their heroes' ages than were the women in earlier Harlequin Romances and Presents. Two of the heroines were virgins at the beginning of the novel, at ages 22 (Mather, 1984) and 25 (Darcy, 1984). However, one heroine was an unwed mother—a first and only among the romances read for this study (Clair, 1984).

The economic and social status differences between hero and heroine usually continued to be pronounced. In Sally Wentworth's *backfire*, Abby Stevens was an out-of-work actress while Lance Lazenby was a holding company executive and owned a chauffered Rolls Royce. The widest difference was between Anne Mather's virginal secretary and her heir to an Arabian Sheikdom (Mather, 1984).

Two heroines were out of work—Wentworth's Abby Stevens (1984) and Flora Kidd's Samantha Clifton (1984). Another heroine, however, was an expert jade carver—Daphne Clair's Alex Cameron (1984). And Emma Darcy's Maggie Tarrington (1984) was not only a workaholic, actually shown at work, but she was admired for that commitment by her workaholic hero.

Noting these as well as other aspects of the Harlequin Presents, these United Kingdom authors seemed, generally speaking, divided between the conservative Mather and Kidd on the one hand, and the more feminist Clair and Darcy on the other, with Wentworth more difficult to categorize. Kidd and Mather were women in their 50s; Emma Darcy was a new author and had published only two Harlequin Presents. Therefore, differences among the romances may have reflected their authors' ages. Pursuing this line of inquiry, all the Presents mentioned feminism, with Kidd writing the most antifeminist novel among all the category romances read for this study. Mather, the most published of Harlequin Enterprises Limited authors, stuck to her sheik-secretary kind of formula, but her book did take chances by covering new sexual ground. Furthermore, her sheik immediately followed his pseudo-rape of the heroine with an apology.

Pointedly, reading these Harlequin Presents after reading American category romances was almost as shocking a departure from reality as Harlequin Romances and Presents seemed to me during my first foray into them in 1977. Presents heroines and heroes flared into antagonism the minute they met; the heroines lusted from first page to last. Although often plucky, heroines tripped a lot. Heroes were less brutal than in 1977, but they threatened rape and punishment often enough. They did apologize for their brutality instead of waiting until the last five pages. But still, they were much more expert at lovemaking than their heroines. For example, Wentworth's Lance "touched [the heroine] expertly, knowing exactly how to rouse her" (Wentworth, 1984: 99). In American categories, protagonists explored and learned together.

Love more often than not was lust in the Kidd and Mather novels: "After having felt passion surge through her. . . . Was it possible [that passion meant] she was still in love with him?" (Kidd, 1984: 59). However, in the most interesting of these five, Darcy's hero had to accept a truly Platonic love ideal in which the two became one person. In the end, he came around as follows: "You are necessary to me. I'm incomplete without you" (Darcy, 1984: 188).

While Mather's hero threatened punishment and the rough kisses of Wentworth's hero could turn his heroine to jelly, the protagonists of Clair and Darcy experienced "almost fierce" and "wild" rather than "brutal" sexuality: "His lovemaking became almost fierce, a demanding, bruising conquest of the senses that finally roused her to a feverish response" (Clair, 1984: 165). Here it was the senses, not the body, that got bruised.

The diversity of the five Harlequin Presents made it fruitful to look at the new ground they covered and their approaches to feminism. Again, among these appeared the first unwed mother. Clair's Alex (short for Alexandra) did not wed the wimpy father of her child who ran away during her pregnancy. She "went up North for a while—you know? To an aunt in Auckland. Well, nine years ago it wasn't quite so—acceptable as now" (80). Alex was unconventional in other ways too, and in the end she and her husband agreed to live separately for a time, seeing each other only on weekends.

Interestingly, one of the "conservative" authors, Anne Mather, produced the first category romance discovered in this study which dealt with a heroine who masturbated a man. As noted above, Mather was possibly the first to write a Harlequin Presents depicting unmarried sex and therefore had shown, with her publisher, a willingness to explore new sexual territory within guided plot lines. This exploration of new sexual territory furthered attempts to make the products of Harlequin Enterprises Limited and other romance publishers even more "sexy." Alan Kreizenbeck noted that a criterion of sexy in soap operas was, "Did it attempt to break new ground either verbally or visually?" (Kreizenbeck, 1983: 175). Obviously, guidelines concerning acceptable sexual activity had changed.

The newly emerging pattern for Harlequin Presents seemed to include rape titillation through fear of rape and the occurence of half-rapes rather than actual rape or threats of rape by heroes. This seemed to reflect readers' responses, as readers found rapacious heroes unacceptable but suggestive sexual scenes attractive. In addition, the new pattern followed trends set by 1977–1978 best-sellers.

Another prevalence was the introduction of feminism into these Harlequin Presents. All five dealt with feminism in some way. For example, jade-carving Alex behaved as a modern woman although she carefully separated "liberated" from "feminist." The most engrossing of these Presents were Kidd's anti-feminist diatribe *passionate pursuit* (1984) and Darcy's very feminist novel *tangle of torment* (1984).

Most telling was Kidd's portrayal of her heroine's supposed rival, the feminist author Morgana Taylor, introduced in a "clinging black gown . . . her dark eyes sending what Samantha [the heroine] had sardonically called 'bedroom messages' to [Craig]" (Kidd, 1984: 34). Later, Morgana had "a long fingered red-tipped hand over Craig's" (99), and exhibited "small cat-like teeth" which "glint[ed]" (101). Toward the end of the novel, Morgana said to Samantha,

"I felt you'd struck a blow on behalf of feminism, refusing to be domineered over by [Craig]. But I'd have thought by now you'd have gone ahead and divorced him and taken what you could from him in the way of a good settlement" (157).

And, finally, Morgana apparently pushed the heroine down a flight of stairs (160).

Markedly different was Darcy's *tangle of torment*. The heroine, Maggie, who had a "natural facility for mathematics" (Darcy, 1984: 15), made her most feminist speech while attempting to fend off her villain-fiancé. "I'm not a possession, Dan. . . . I have the right [to go on with my work] without any concession from you" (88). However, like so many heroines of Harlequin products she did act like a wimp toward the end. Her hero, Ian, had finally popped the question, and "then reason whispered that he was intent on the role of father, not husband. Being a husband to her was incidental" (179). She could "reason" this way because they had had sexual intercourse once, and it had resulted in pregnancy. Nevertheless, Ian was androgynous. He did visit "almost" brutal kisses upon her (103) and even a punishing kiss which turned sexy (104), but she was the one who pursued him and he was the unwilling party. On page 178 came a first: "His hands lifted and fell in a hopeless little gesture." Heroes never made "hopeless" much less "little" gestures in older Harlequin Presents or Romances. And as noted above, not only would Maggie continue her career after marriage, but Ian accepted that he was incomplete without her, saying the kinds of things only heroines had said in the older romances.

As in the past, many heroines gave more than they got in the end. Mather's Rachel not only married her sheik-to-be, she would live with him in Bahdan, a desert country she hated at first sight. In a somewhat typical evasion of the career-versus-marriage issue, Kidd's Craig said, "I wouldn't like [your going back to work], but I wouldn't object." To which she confessed " 'I . . . I don't think [I'll take the job]' " (Kidd, 1984: 188). He did make concessions, however. He would cut down on the amount of time he had been spending on his business, and they needn't live all year in Canada, a place that she disliked. Instead, they would spend "winter in the Caribbean, springtime in England, high summer and early fall in Canada" (187).

Thus 1984 Harlequin Presents reflected some of the changes first found in American category novels. Lovemaking was generally more gentle, and feminism existed, although it certainly wasn't always swallowed with ease. There was a striking discrepancy between authors who dwelt on their heroines' lust and willingness to subsume their identities and authors who portrayed assertive career-oriented heroines.

Since the publishers of Harlequin Enterprises Limited made a concerted effort to appeal to American readers, these changes in the Presents line probably indicated once again that the American audience increasingly expected gentle, communicative heroes and career-oriented but sensual heroines. Furthermore, in the spring of

1984, a look at the shelves of Toronto bookstores indicated that the publisher was right to pursue these trends for Canadian women as well. Prominently displayed were multitudes of Silhouette Books; the local product was almost nowhere to be found (Frenier visit).

CATEGORY ROMANCES IMMEDIATELY AFTER THE ROMANCE WARS

Sales of category romances, and in particular those published by Harlequin Enterprises Limited, reached their peak in 1982. The profits of Harlequin Enterprises Limited fell from $22 million in 1982 to $10 million in 1983. The publisher "blamed the drop in operating profit on increased competition in the romance market and a resulting rise in returns" ("Harlequin," 1984: 29). However, in August 1984, Harlequin Enterprises Limited took over the distribution of Silhouette Books (Lazare, 1987: 2; Reuter, 1984: 16).

This market shift followed the proliferation of romance lines which had begun in May 1980. As ever steamier American lines became popular, "sweet" lines like Bantam's Circle of Love— launched in January 1982—failed to sell, and sexy lines like Dell's Candlelight Ecstasy rose to the top.

In the process, however, "the sexy angle . . . was losing its luster," and many readers began seeking alternative forms of romance, such as historical romances, regencies, and traditional mysteries (Jennings, 1984: 54). Nevertheless, by 1985 the most popular category romance lines were Velvet Glove, a sexy line published by Avon, and Loveswept, a sometimes sexy line, by Bantam Books. The other most popular lines downplayed sexuality: Silhouette Romance, Harlequin American Romance, and Harlequin Temptation. All five of these bestselling lines featured American authors.

In this more polarized offering, the most popular lines could finally be raunchy. For example, " 'Damn, if that's what you think, you've never gone to the gym with him,' Bernie muttered. 'The King's got a scepter that's eleven inches' " (Holder, 1985: 2). Still, even with this license, heroes did not kiss punishingly nor did they grip brutally. Instead, heroines as well as heroes kissed "hungrily" or "thirstily."

More importantly, in these sexier books most heroines were not virgins at the beginning of the story. Furthermore, their lack of virginity was seen neither as extraordinary nor as reprehensible by the heroes. In addition to this reduced sexual double standard—and like their egalitarian 1984 predecessors—these newest heroines were older and held jobs or pursued careers, although they still meant to combine career, marriage, and motherhood. Underlining this change, some "bad" women were shown as lazy for not wanting to work outside the home (Michael, 1984).

As heroines became more feminist, so did heroes. They remained sensitive and relatively ordinary men; few were Arabian sheiks or Greek shipping tycoons. At times, plots depicted distinct gender role-reversals. For example, in Jenna Lee Joyce's *Wintersfield*, the farmer heroine was a widow and mother who taught the hero to farm.

The most important innovation was that the readers were at last let into the hero's thoughts about his own overt sexuality:

I need to see you, he thought desperately. *All of you, without that robe and frilly nightgown. I need to be inside you.* He clutched the newspaper desperately, not daring to move for fear the rubbing of his slacks would tip him beyond control (McCaffree, 1984: 151, author's italics).

As heroes' thoughts about their own sexuality were depicted, and as references to their erections became a craze, heroes seemed more vulnerable than ever before in category romances. And as heroes seemed more vulnerable, heroines appeared more powerful.

Adding to this, feminism was mentioned in the vast majority of these romances; this time as authors and their protagonists seemed to come to terms with a version of the new gender roles of the 1980s. However, the now less powerful heroes still retained superior sway in sexual encounters, even when "feminist" heroines initiated sex or even proposed marriage, as in Martha Starr's *From Twilight to Sunrise* (Starr, 1984: 222).

Also telling, although heroes continued to make important compromises in the interest of their marital relationships, these newest romances depicted heroines who believed in dropping their careers—temporarily, to be sure—while they raised children. This was in contrast to the more egalitarian 1984 romances which did not dwell on this kind of career delay. In addition, none of these 1985 romances suggested that a marriage could survive long periods of geographic separation. Finally, a poignant example of ambiguity crept into several of the newest American romances. These counselled that, since some heroes were unable to express tender feelings, their heroines must be patient. For example, in Joyce's *Wintersfield*, the heroine finally discovered that the hero loved her, but he had trouble telling her so. She talked with her mother.

"It took me ten years to get that kind of information out of your father." [Her mother's] voice softened with the memory. "Patience is a virtue," she advised. "Let Travis explain himself to you in his own good time, and you'll never regret it" (Joyce, 1985: 212).

As did American society, by 1985 romances had grappled with changing expectations of women. Role-reversal was shown as desirable in some areas of daily life; career women were seen as admirable so long as they did not eschew marriage and were willing, unlike their husbands, to temporarily abandon career for early parenthood. Most tellingly, sensitive and nurturant heroes were depicted as the most desirable of men, even though they were sometimes permitted to retain 1950-era machismo, and though they always remained ultimately dominant in sexual scenes.

ROMANCES RESPOND TO THE REAGAN ERA

Popular culture reacts to societal change more than it shapes it; furthermore, publishers of romances tend to be conservative in a primary sense: slow to change. But, in the 1980s, America experienced a wave of a new kind of "conservatism" which translated into a renewed puritanism about sexual matters. This stemmed from concern that the 1970s sexual revolution had resulted in high rates of teenage sexual activity and pregnancy and the highest rate of divorce in the nation's history in 1982. Then the modern plague struck. By summer 1987, the Surgeon General of the United States could be seen on television making public service announcements warning Americans to refrain from "unsafe sex." By then, romances also began to respond to these 1980s concerns.

During spring 1987, readers first chose romances on the basis of their authors. When they exhausted the supply of books by their favorites, they chose those published by Zebra, a non-category publisher. Next came category romances published by Loveswept, followed by Silhouette Intimate Moments and Silhouette Romances.

These romances remained especially popular in rural America. In April 1987, the assistant manager at the St. Cloud B. Dalton store, recently transferred from the Southdale store in Minneapolis, noted that romance sales were still higher in areas like St. Cloud (a small city of 42,000) than in cities like Minneapolis–St. Paul (part of a total metropolitan population of over 2 million). In fact, the store in St. Cloud employed two romance experts; how purposefully I could not determine. That romance sales, although still of vital importance, were down compared to their peak in the early 1980s meant multiple sales gimmicks for romance readers. These included A Frequent Buyer Bonus Plan and a copy of "Whispers: A Publication of the B. Dalton Romance Book Club." A sign of failure followed in July 1987 when I received a notice addressed to "Dear B. Dalton Book Club Member: or Frequent Buyer Participant:" which said, "the overall interest generated in these programs was not as great as we anticipated. . . . Therefore, all B. Dalton Book Clubs and the B. Dalton Frequent Buyer Bonus Plan are discontinued effective June 30, 1987" ("Important Announcement," 1987).

Nevertheless, many book racks—in St. Cloud and every other rural midwestern B. Dalton I visited—still displayed romances indicating that while business might be down, it certainly wasn't out. Following the advice of the St. Cloud assistant manager, I purchased May 1987s crop of Loveswept (four), Silhouette Intimate Moments (four), and Silhouette Romance (six). Still sexy in content, the Loveswept covers sported two heroines in long sleeves and only one in a décolleté dress. This seemed an exterior response to concerns expressed at the June 1986 Romance Writers of America Convention where the issue of censorship was paramount. Intimate Moments covers showed lustier couples but with only one bared chest—his. The super-chaste Silhouette Romance covers could have graced 1970 Harlequin Romances.

All the heroines of these books were employed at the beginnings of the romances. Their occupations varied from a widowed mother of two who typed at home (Pickart, 1987) to the most overtly feminist heroine, Brenda Trent's Glenna Johnson, a firefighter (Trent, 1987). Evidently none of the heroines had had sexual experiences outside of marriage, in any case, previous sexual experience went unaddressed; there were four divorcées and two widows. But what really interested me was the stress on virginity in two Silhouette Romances: Pepper Adam's heroine was a virgin at 25 (Adams, 1987) as was the 24-year-old heroine of England-born Valerie Parv (Parv, 1987). Noticeably, the average age of the heroines (where given) varied from 23 1/2 in the Silhouette Romances to 28 1/2 in the Silhouette Intimate Moments. The heroes' ages varied from almost 33 (Silhouette Romances) to 36 1/2 (Loveswept). None of the heroines was the same age as her hero, much less older than he. That is, while heroines were older in 1987 than in 1977, they again paired with men considerably older than themselves.

This retreat from reality joined a retreat from attempts at raunchy sexuality. However, some of the Loveswept and Silhouette Intimate Moments still steamed mightily. Raven Anderson, 28-year-old Federal Agent—read spy—finally bedded with Joshua Long, 35-year-old super-wealthy owner of hotels and an airline:

And when his mouth at last closed hotly on her nipple. . . .
She could feel his hand moving down her hip, then skim tantalizingly up the inside of one thigh. . . . He couldn't take his eyes off her tense, striving face, watching her faint, jerky movements. . . .
He had managed to rein his desperate need (Hooper, 1987: 107).

As before, gentle lovemaking predominated, cruel sexual encounters had long since disappeared. Operative terms remained "hungry" and "thirsty," possessive rather than brutal or bruising. While heroes dominated in most such encounters, a few heroines initiated sex. Jessie Wentworth, 29-year-old manager of Wentworth Enterprises, began her first sexual meeting with Blake Montgomery, college professor and traveling magician: "Without thinking she lifted her lips to his. . . . His tongue plunged. . . . He hauled her close. . . . She kissed him mindlessly" (Webb, 1987: 49). However, either the assertive heroine was unthinking like Jessie or otherwise inept. A Silhouette Romance heroine, super-virginal Maggie Ryan, 25-year-old receptionist, was mousey and initially considered so by her hero J. P. Tucker, 34, Secret Service Agent. Supremely clumsy, she blurted out "You sure are cute" (Adams, 1987: 35). " 'I would have danced with you.' She smiled invitingly. 'But you didn't ask. Why didn't you?' " (36). Later, " 'Well, if nothing is wrong, will you kindly tell me what happened? One minute you're kissing my breasts and the next minute you're not. Did you encounter something unpleasant?' " (124).

In this last example, these protagaonists pursued the bad people—a villainess included—together. Likewise, other heroines no longer strange to heroes's careers often worked with them solving mysteries, in two Loveswepts, one Silhouette Intimate Moments, and one Silhouette Romance (*Across the River of Yesterday*, *Raven on the Wing*, *Bayou Midnight*, and *It Takes a Thief*). Many heroines continued careers, although the reader had to hunt to discover the continuance as it was much down-played compared to 1984 romances. Some heroines made "traditional" choices the widowed Courtney Marshall, mother of two, gave up her home typing to move in with Luke Hamilton and become his homemaker, but—in part reflecting 1970s changes—not his maid. Hero:

"You're not a maid!"
"No, I'm a wife, a mother, a homemaker. That's who I am, what I am. That's what brings me infinite joy. Let me do what I do best" (Pickart, 1987: 178).

All six Silhouette Romance heroines ended with careers of their own or would work in conjunction with their husbands—farm or run a business together. The heroines of the Silhouette Intimate Moments all kept their careers, although three of them never experienced any career-relationship conflict at all. Only the jobs of the sexy Loveswept heroines were likely to dissipate as love and marriage changed their lives; however, the heroine with the highest status of all, Loveswept's Jessie Wentworth, continued to run her department store as her hero joined her to run its children's department (Webb, 1987). All in all, careers were generally assumed and seldom abandoned—a clear turnabout from the 1970s—even though the importance of work outside the home was deemphasised compared to 1984.

The two romances written by non-American authors again illustrated the differences between the American and United Kingdom products as well as the penetration of the women's movement into American women's popular culture. The heroine of *The Leopard Tree*, set in Australia and written by Valerie Parv (born in England), thought briefly that her hero was from outerspace. But the plot quickly veered to a concern with her villainous, rape-threatening fiancé and displays of her tripping ineptness. Nevertheless, this was the sexiest of the Silhouette Romances, involving torrid petting (Parv, 1987: 121) and even a "wet dreaming" (my term) heroine (67). The more interesting Lucy Gordon's *A Pearl Beyond Price* paired an orphaned 22-year-old virgin-widow English nurse with a 34-year-old Italian millionare. "Mrs." Lynette Hallam—the American authors used "Ms."—drank sherry, Renato Bardini, brandy. He imprisoned her in his Italian mansion-home and so forth. However, not only was the petting in this romance heavy, this heroine was more assertive than her 1970 or 1977 counterparts and antagonism between the protagonists abated by pages 103–4, leaving 80 pages for them to come more gently together.

In contrast, American heroines and heroes never had such hackneyed plots nor such wide status or age differences. In addition, American authors enjoyed playing with more role reversals than ever before. These could occur during love-making. Joshua Long to Raven Anderson: "You never touch me unless you want me. . . . Only when we've made love and your defenses are still down" (Hooper, 1987: 139; see also Johansen, 1987: 99). There were, as well, more general examples:

[Gideon Brandt] stood up with the leashed ferocity of a caged leopard. "You've been a fantastic lover, but I need more than sex. I need you to trust me and let me become a part of you. Sex isn't enough and I won't let you use it as a substitute." He turned to the door (Johansen, 111).

Whereas all studies indicate that the American woman is likely to find her men equating love with sex, Gideon and Josh accused their heroines of this attitude. Furthermore, it is of note that Gideon's leashed ferocity, while still delineating "masculinity," did not result in abuse of his heroine.

The most notable role reversal involved Maggie Ryan, heroine of *In Hot Pursuit*, who let J. P. Tucker believe they had had coitus when he passed out (Adams, 1987: 162). Furthermore, she proposed marriage to him (186). Also of note, while now heroes were not especially schizophrenic, two heroines were (*Across the River of Yesterday* and *A Pearl Beyond Price*).

Old concepts were further reversed as when "homes" were now associated with American heroines and loneliness with heroes; this was true even in the novel set in Australia. And heroines were at least, if not more, perceptive than heroes (see especially Pickart, 1987: 107–08; and Richards, 1987: 82). Most American heroines not only held down careers or jobs, they usually did not trip and were far more intelligent and less overly personalizing than heroines of years previous to 1984.

Generally, 1987 heroines were less independent than those of 1984 and 1985; as noted, their sexuality was confined to marriage and their careers were less important to them. Nevertheless, these 1987 women experienced sexuality that always began gently, rather often became "fierce," "rough," "possessive," but never brutal. The hero ultimately controlled sexuality as "he plundered" and "she followed." However, in the sexier books, foreplay was never neglected and almost always involved licked breasts followed by either his masturbation of her (as above in *Raven on the Wing*) or more likely cunnilingus and less often fellatio. "She slid down his body, searing his throat, his nipples, his navel with her tongue. He ached. She moved lower, her mouth closing around him. He exploded" (Webb, 1987: 148).

Amidst all this, birth control was never mentioned, even when the illegitimate hero would not copulate with his heroine for fear she might become pregnant (Adams, 1987: 109). Coitus occurred in these romances before marriage but almost always after a marriage proposal. And, all these ended with marriage—in a romantic alleviation of American women's new concerns about commitment if not about safe sex. In fact, usually heroes wanted marriage at least as much if not more than heroines (see especially Hooper 1987; Rainville, 1987, and Ferrell, 1987).

Feminism in 1987 still shone forth in the behavior of heroines; they had careers, assisted with mystery solving, and were intelligent and perceptive. More assertive, some heroines had legitimate power. Most overtly, theatrical agent Aurora Fields "extended her hand, but stayed behind her desk. It was, she'd learned, important to establish certain positions of power right from the start" (Roberts, 1987: 190). However, heroines usually relied on traditional power. For example, that new perceptiveness—as Aurora was blessed with psychic powers—David Brady said to her, "A man has to wonder if he'll have any secrets from a woman who can look inside him" (131), and more traditional power: "He remembered the way she looked when they made love—slim, glowing and as dangerous as a neutron bomb" (159).

However, in the most anti-feminist of the novels, *Wild Poppies*, feminism was merely sexual revolution as the hero worried that the widowed heroine could not cope with the new "singles dating scene." "[T]here are women who ask men out, then pick up the tab for the entire evening," Luke told Courtney (Pickart, 1987: 39) and as noted before this heroine used feminism for traditional ends: " 'I've discovered exactly who I am . . . a wife, a mother, a homemaker' " (87).

The most overtly feminist heroine wanted to be a firefighter in a small southern town. Beginning her first firefighting job, she unprofessionally flared out at her captain-hero (Trent, 1987: 23–24). Whereas, he was the true feminist:

He toyed with the handle of his coffee cup and tried to think of some tactful way to handle this situation. Here was the opportunity to move on from this point and behave with [the heroine] like a captain should with any new recruit (90–91).

All in all, 1987 American category romances represented grass roots incorporations of some of the 1980s backlash reaction to the 1970s sexual revolution and women's movement. Societally, pre-marital sexuality did not disappear, but it was more often associated with engagement and marriage. Careers did not disappear, but feminists as well as other segments of society expressed concerns about combining them with family.

In romances, toned-down sex meant less ribald phrasing, fewer scenes of coitus, and marriage or imminent marriage. However, ever lengthening petting scenes remained heated and oral sex occurred more often and more explicitly than ever. Romance heroines concentrated less on careers but assumed them as part of their existence just as they assumed marriage and children. Heroines did continue to ignore the burden of the double job that would ensue. Rather like their heroes, these women would romantically "have it all" with great ease. As to those heroes, they remained sensitive and feminist in their behaviors toward heroines while becoming ever more terrific in bed.

7

Conclusion

In the 1970s and 1980s, as the governments of the United Kingdom and the United States began implementing legal changes to equalize the status of females, and as increasing numbers of women voted, worked outside the home, and entered institutions of higher education, the popularity of women's romances boomed. Why?

First, popular culture responds to a general need for fantasy and escape, and probably this need is exaggerated as people enter an increasingly fast-paced and changing world complicated by new gender-role expectations (Agena, 1983: 66; Campbell, 1984: 72). In addition, most women who work outside the home face two full-time jobs, one unpaid and one underpaid. From 1970 to 1987, many of these women sought outlets by reading romances. Some of these readers may also have sought heroines who either solved the dilemma of holding two jobs or the increasingly few who evaded it entirely; in the 1970s and 1980s, romances provided such heroines. In addition, romances changed to depict ever more realizable fantasies in other ways as well.

As heroines changed, depictions of heroes as the other, controls over the heroines' sexuality, and the nature of the heroines' powers altered even more. The first change came in response to the sexual revolution of the 1960s and 1970s, and involved portrayals of lusting, though virginal, heroines who had to be contained by every more powerful, and ever more brutal, protective heroes. However, with the entry of American authors into the genre in the early 1980s, more egalitarian and tender heroes were introduced and then became a commonplace. These heroes, ever more nurturant, remained adequate protectors even as the status differences between protagonists became less distinct. In this most important way, the category romance hero came to fulfill romance readers' "ideal," as discovered by Janice Radway. In addition, by the mid-1980s, these self-revealing heroes were more vulnerable than ever before in category romances.

Accompanying these shifts, as "feminism" ceased to be a pejorative, hero and heroine were likely to behave in a feminist fashion. Although the hero remained dominant in the bedroom, even that dominance continually lessened.

In the economic sphere, heroines seldom permanently gave up career or job for marriage; usually they assumed their careers much as their heroes had all along. Importantly, heroes as well as heroines either made compromises about work situations, geographic location, and lifestyles for the sake of their heterosexual relationships, or these matters were of no concern whatsoever.

Thus, while I agree with Modleski that women's romances are about women's power, significant shifts in women's power had occurred; by the late 1980s, heroes had emerged as less powerful and heroines as more powerful than at any time before 1984–1985. Heroines' sexual independence waivered but that of heroes lessened and assumptions about the heroines' careers seemed irreversible.

With the arrival of a higher level of egalitarianism, controls over women's sexuality had to be shifted and the nature of lust had to be redefined. Whereas lust had been covert and unmentionable in 1970, it became the foremost topic of the most popular category romances by 1977, thanks to market demand. Differentiating lust from love became their story pivot, as it became the task of the heroine—and secondarily of the hero—to distinguish between the two. In perhaps the most anguished response to perceived male flight from commitment, by 1977 authors were beginning to overtly portray heroes as the victims of their overwhelming lust for and love of heroines. And those heroines were lusty enough to keep their heroes sexually satisfied and monogamous forever.

Again, the entry of American authors altered the treatment of lust as well as the portrayal of heroes and of heroine power. By the early 1980s, ordinary lust no longer inevitably lead to marriage. However, extraordinary lust remained equated with perpetual monogamy, and presumably marriage, for hero and heroine. In addition, while heroes were tender in behavior—often sensitive even to the point of blushing—some were "patronizingly" assisted by their brides to verbalize tender feelings. By the mid-1980s, extraordinary lust remained associated with monogamy but most heroines had never experienced the ordinary variety at all. In the late 1980s, even as heroines reverted to pre-marital virginity, heroes continued to become ever more sensitive, understanding, and androgynous. In these various ways, "traditional" women were reflected through the 1960s sexual revolution, the 1970s feminist movement, and the 1980s conservative backlash. Furthermore, heroines had not only gained more economic power and, over the whole period, more overt personal power; in addition, they were able to permanently attach the roaming heroes of the 1980s.

Over the years, some of the changes in categories undermined the coping 1950s woman, especially as they came to fondly portray career women who enjoyed their economic independence and behaved, talked, and thought in feminist ways. But romances continued to uphold that woman by rewarding her with the myth of a hero obsessed with his heroine. Thus by the late 1980s, category romances satisfied the world view of that proportion of American women who might have been sympathetic to American anti-abortion activists (Luker, 1984; Ginsburg, 1984). Interpreting a 1980 survey of a random sample of members of the pro-life National Right to Live Committee, Ginsburg noted,

Contrary to popular stereotypes of pro-life activists, . . . respondents are not anti-feminist on many issues. Ninety percent do not agree that women "should leave running the country up to men" and 83 percent approve of women working regardless of marital status and husband's income. . . . If women perceive legal abortion as a threat, it is because it represents public acceptance of the possibility that female sexuality need not be tied inevitably to motherhood. In so doing, abortion also serves to weaken social pressure on men to take responsibility for the reproductive consequences of intercourse (Ginsburg, 1984: 182–83).

Mid- and late-1980s romances agreed with anti-abortion activists that heroines could have careers but should also permanently at-

tach their heroes to themselves. Like those activists, romances in
the long run tied their heroines' sexuality to marriage, but unlike
them, the tie with motherhood was tenuous. In fact, as romances
changed, their modernized protagonists engaged in explicitly described sexuality for the sake of sexuality, not procreation. Thus,
while sticking pretty well to some conservative ideals, romances
had changed in a fundamentally unconservative way in order to
sell to the larger market. In this last process, were romances becoming "unromantic" by veering off the old formula that constituted romance and becoming "soft porn" for women?

I have cited feminist critics of romances who found Harlequin
Romances (used as a generic) "pornographic." Following is a def-
inition of pornography worked out by anti-pornography feminists
Andrea Dworkin and Catharine MacKinnon.

Women presented as sexual objects, things or commodities, who enjoy
pain or humiliation, who experience sexual pleasure in being raped, who
are tied up or cut up or mutilated or bruised or physically hurt; women
who are presented in postures of sexual submission; women's body parts
are exhibited such that women are reduced to those parts; women are
presented as whores by nature; women are penetrated by objects or animals, or women are presented in scenarios of degradation, injury, abase-
ment, torture, shown as filthy or inferior, bleeding or hurt in a context
that makes these conditions sexual; or the use of men, children, or trans-
sexuals in the place of women in the above (Allen, 1983: 10A).

The reporter Martha S. Allen asked about these criteria: "Would
Manet's famous painting of Luncheon on the Grass . . . be pornographic? How about *Vogue*? *Playboy*? the Harlequin Romances? *Hustler*?" (Allen, 1983: 10A).

The older Harlequins and some of the 1984 Harlequins represented "Women . . . who enjoy pain or humiliation . . . who are
. . . bruised or physically hurt . . . are presented as . . . inferior,
. . . or hurt in a context that makes these conditions sexual."
However, the majority of American category romances and even
some sexy mid-1980s products of Harlequin Enterprises Limited
did not portray such women. In addition, American romance heroines did not act like battered women, and they responded to wild
rather than punishing lovemaking.

The other concern—were romances becoming "unromantic" in the sense of too realistic?—is not only harder to address, ultimately the answer just isn't in yet. Marilyn M. Lowery, author of *How to Write Romance Novels That Sell*, wondered about this problem. As editors asked for more realism, she worried, "Veering too far from fantasy may diminish the romantic aura" (Lowery, 1983: 54). In addition, John G. Cawelti, the foremost cultural theoretician of formula stories, pointed out, "If a character becomes too complexly human he may cast a shattering and disruptive light on the other elements of the formula" (Cawelti, 1976: 12).

Is it romantic to describe children with their varied problems as in the To Have and To Hold series? Is a concern over birth control methods romantic (some best-sellers and categories presented this concern in the early 1980s)? Most important, can a heroine who exerts overt power be romantic?

As noted above, romance has mythic proportions; that is why it appeals. According to Will Wright, "Myth depends on simple and recognizable meanings which reinforce rather than challenge social understanding. For this purpose, a structure of oppositions is necessary" (Wright, 1975: 23). In the older category romances, men and women were opposites. Action revolved around their antagonism. In the newer romances, the protagonists were often more realistically portrayed and therefore more alike than unlike, and antagonism was subsumed to their movements toward understanding themselves and each other. Compared to earlier romances, a more powerful heroine mated with a less powerful hero; they weren't as opposite anymore. However, as Wright also pointed out, "Myths are easily understood, conceptually deep, and socially relevant; they reflect and reveal basic concerns and directions of their society. They may also model the fundamental approaches to the meaning and ordering of experiences available to human consciousness" (194). Newer category romances did adhere to this definition of myth. They modeled approaches, gave guidelines, and ordered experiences. The question remains, however: did these romances fulfill their readers' need for myth?

Intriguingly, a partial answer can be gleaned from the fact that by February 1986 my local public library no longer obstructed its aisles with kiosks displaying romances. Local booksellers stocked far fewer of them than at the genre's height in 1982–1984. In fact, our most old-fashioned drug store now stocked—alongside a few tame category and many steamy best-selling romances—Beeline Classics: "hard porn" books the size and shape of Harlequin Romances (meant to sell and mostly selling to men). Gentler, more egalitarian romances sold well for a while, but American women got bored with them and became more pluralistic in their book buying habits.

Will romances, emulating history, become popular once again? If so, when and why? Will readers merely get over their boredom with love stories, or will they again want to escape from stresses in their personal and work lives by returning to formulaic romance?

In answer to the other questions posed in the introduction and by other feminist students of this genre, the newer category romances and bestselling romances varied in their portrayals of heroine independence or dependence. The trend in category romances—as distinct from best-sellers—seemed to be toward independent career women more emotionally dependent on their husbands. Obviously, many heroines no longer used their career independence as a mere ploy.

Heroes tended to be more sensitive, loving, communicative, and far less nasty in the newer books. Thus the new romances acted less to soothe ambivalence (a concern of Ann Barr Snitow); they seldom turned rape into love. Perhaps they did less than older romances to heal the tensions between the discrimination against and the adulation of women that readers still find in their real world.

More realistic than the heroes, heroines were hiding their sexual impulses less than in older romances, and could enjoy sanctioned sex before marriage. Consequently, marriages were only partially based on the sexual power of heroines. Most new heroines had to have additional attractions—empathy for their heroes, a positive attitude toward their own career—as well as the standard ones: loyalty to their heroes and love of children.

All forms of sado-masochism became less acceptable and American categories were never manuals on how to become a battered wife. While heroes remained dominant in bed, they became less so than ever before. But the new, more egalitarian sex began to sell less well too, as all category romances began to sell less well by 1985.

Romances continued to compromise the reader as she identified with the heroine and tried to see herself and the heroine with men's eyes. With the trend toward expressing the hero's point of view, this may have been further complicated, especially since the hero's thoughts were written by women authors. These newly sensitive heroes who were obsessed by thoughts of love for their heroines were not like real American men who remained job- and ego-oriented, rather than relationship-oriented as real American women were (see Bernard, 1973; and Ehrenreich, 1983).

Consequently, these new romances continued to reinforce American women's unrealistic views of men. Nor did they give realistic portrayals of long-term heterosexual relationships. More pleasant to read because more erotic and less sado-masochist, mid- and late-1980s romances were still escapist fantasies pushing unrealizable relationships involving men the likes of whom are rare in real life.

As to whether these newer romances were regressive fantasies fueled by readers' memories of security in infancy, I have hinted at my discomfort with this particular analysis of romances. But I am aware that they tap into what Stanton Peele in his *Love and Addiction* called addictive love—that is, love that can't be done without. This love causes withdrawal anxiety when it ceases to be reciprocated, and is tied to concepts of safety (Peele, 1975: Schaef, 1986).

I note that, unlike tobacco, alcohol, and hard drugs, which are seen as negative addictions, romantic love is still seen as a positive one in our culture. These romances, and much of our popular culture, teach that jealousy and possessiveness are characteristics of true love; that true love is monogamous and usually comes once in a lifetime; that such love means two become one instead of remaining separate people emotionally; and that separation should cause withdrawal symptoms. Old Harlequin Romances hid their portrayals of addicted lovers beneath virginal girls devoted to conquering heroes. By the late 1970s, Harlequin Romances and Presents lauded addictive love even as their protagonists moved away from the trappings of so-called traditional gender roles. The 1980s romances were more "modern" in that they portrayed heroines who sought career independence, but these heroines remained addicted to heroes who were addicted to them.

In all this, the basic appeal of these romances remained their display of heroine power. While the status differences between heroine and hero were less marked in the newer romances, the heroine retained her ability to enthrall a hero. The attraction of addictive love was to get someone addicted to her, and 1980s heroines continued to manage that trick in romance after romance.

I do depart from Kay Mussell's assertion that "female passivity in romantic relationships" had "not faded or significantly altered" in the new romances (1984: xii). Instead, I see the beginnings of portrayals of sexually assertive heroines who were starting to ask for more equal treatment in their relationships with heroes. As pointed out above, this meant that couples by the late 1980s often united their direct powers in pursuit of the same adventure. This was already happening in the popular Velvet Glove line by 1985.

Still popular with rural American women, the heroines of late 1980s American category romances lusted and adventured. Their heroes enjoyed their lust, accepted their work outside the home, appreciated their detecting abilities, and still remained addicted to them. Powerful heroines? Traditional only partly; romantic, probably; powerful, no question.

Bibliography

PRIMARY SOURCES

Candlelight Ecstasy Romances

Andrews, Barbara. *Midnight Magic*. New York: Dell Publishing, Feb. 1984.

Copeland, Lori. *All or Nothing*. New York: Dell Publishing, Feb. 1984.

Graham, Heather. *Tender Deception*. New York: Dell Publishing, Feb. 1984.

Hale, Antoinette. *Trouble in Paradise*. New York: Dell Publishing, April 1984.

Herber, Lori. *All Our Tomorrows*. New York: Dell Publishing, Feb. 1984.

Lacy, Tira. *Only for Love*. New York: Dell Publishing, March 1984.

Tyler, Alison. *Business Before Pleasure*. New York: Dell Publishing, April 1984.

Whettenburg, Karen. *Winds of Heaven*. New York: Dell Publishing, Feb. 1984.

Candlelight Ecstasy Supreme

Black, Jackie. *Payment in Full*. New York: Dell Publishing, Feb. 1984.

Bryan, Eileen. *Crossfire*. New York: Dell Publishing, Feb. 1984.

Hudson, Anna. *Body and Soul*. New York: Dell Publishing, Feb. 1984.

Hughes, Samantha. *Politics of Passion*. New York: Dell Publishing, Dec. 1983.

Kincaid, Nell. *Where There's Smoke.* New York: Dell Publishing, Feb. 1984.
Vitek, Donna Kemel. *Never Look Back.* New York: Dell Publishing, Dec. 1983.

Harlequin American Romance

Bretton, Barbara. *Love Changes.* Toronto: Harlequin Books, April 1983.
Coffaro, Katherine. *Sunward Journey.* Toronto: Harlequin Books, Dec. 1984.
Flanders, Rebecca. *Daydreams.* Toronto: Harlequin Books, Dec. 1984.
———. *A Matter of Trust.* Toronto: Harlequin Books, May 1983.
———. *Twice in a Lifetime.* Toronto: Harlequin Books, Jan. 1983.
Kitt, Sandra. *Adam and Eva.* Toronto: Harlequin Books, Jan. 1985.
Seidel, Kathleen Gilles. *The Same Last Name.* Toronto: Harlequin Books, April 1983.
Sommers, Beverly. *Mix and Match.* Toronto: Harlequin Books, Jan. 1985.
Starr, Martha. *From Twilight to Sunrise.* Toronto: Harlequin Books, Dec. 1984.
Weger, Jackie. *A Strong and Tender Thread.* Toronto: Harlequin Books, first printing March 1983.
Welles, Caron. *Raven's Song.* Toronto: Harlequin Books, July 1983.

Harlequin Presents

Bauling, Jayne. *wait for the storm.* Toronto: Harlequin Books, June 1982.
Clair, Daphne. *the loving trap.* Toronto: Harlequin Books, June 1982.
———. *a ruling passion.* Toronto: Harlequin Books, April 1984.
Cooper, Ann. *battle with desire.* Toronto: Harlequin Books, 1979.
Dailey, Janet. *heart of stone.* Toronto: Harlequin Books, 1980.
Darcy, Emma. *tangle of torment.* Toronto: Harlequin Books, April 1984.
Hampson, Anne. *south of capricorn.* Toronto: Harlequin Books, June 1982.
Hilton, Margery. *snow bride.* Toronto: Harlequin Books, 1979.
Jordan, Penny. *northern sunset.* Toronto: Harlequin Books, June 1982.
Kidd, Flora. *passionate pursuit.* Toronto: Harlequin Books, April 1984.
Lamb, Charlotte. *call back yesterday.* Toronto: Harlequin Books, 1978.
———. *dark dominion.* Toronto: Harlequin Books, 1979; rept. 1980.
———. *a frozen fire.* Toronto: Harlequin Books, 1980.
Lindsay, Rachel. *love and no marriage.* Toronto: Harlequin Books, 1980.
Mather, Anne. *images of love.* Toronto: Harlequin Books, 1980.
———. *sirocco.* Toronto: Harlequin Books, April 1984.

———. *smokescreen*. Toronto: Harlequin Books, June 1982.

Mortimer, Carole. *fear of love*. Toronto: Harlequin Books, 1980.

———. *love's duel*. Toronto: Harlequin Books, June 1982.

———. *savage interlude*. Toronto: Harlequin Books, 1979.

Seale, Sara. *to catch a unicorn*. Toronto: Harlequin Books, 1964, 9th printing, June 1980.

Wentworth, Sally. *backfire*. Toronto: Harlequin Books, April 1984.

Winspear, Violet. *love is the honey*. Toronto: Harlequin Books, 1980.

———. *the sheik's captive*. Toronto: Harlequin Books, 1979.

Harlequin Romances (Sexy)

Ashton, Elizabeth. *Reluctant Partnership*. Toronto: Harlequin Books, 1979.

Graham, Elizabeth. *New Man at Cedar Hills*. Toronto: Harlequin Books, 1978.

Pargeter, Margaret. *A Man Called Cameron*. Toronto: Harlequin Books, 1978.

Wentworth, Sally. *Liberated Lady*. Toronto: Harlequin Books, 1979.

Whittal, Yvonne. *Bitter Enchantment*. Toronto: Harlequin Books, 1979.

Harlequin Romances (Tame)

Burchell, Mary. *Nightingales*. Toronto: Harlequin Books, 1980.

Neels, Betty. *Last April Fair*. Toronto: Harlequin Books, 1980.

Harlequin Temptation

Bloom, Jill. *Two of a Kind*. Toronto: Harlequin Books, Dec. 1984.

Canon, Mary. *How the Game Is Played*. Toronto: Harlequin Books, Dec. 1984.

Joyce, Jenna Lee. *Wintersfield*. Toronto: Harlequin Books, Dec. 1984.

McCaffree, Sharon. *One Bright Morning*. Toronto: Harlequin Books, Nov. 1984.

Loveswept

Barrett, Elizabeth. *Tailor-Made*. Toronto: Bantam Books, Jan. 1985.

Boswell, Barbara. *Sensuous Perception*. Toronto: Bantam Books, Jan. 1985.

Green, Billie. *The Count from Wisconsin*. Toronto: Bantam Books, Jan. 1985.

Holder, Nancy. *Finders Keepers*. Toronto: Bantam Books, Jan. 1985.
Hooper, Kay. *Raven on the Wing*. Toronto: Bantam Books, May 1987.
Johansen, Iris. *Across the River of Yesterday*. Toronto: Bantam Books, May 1987.
Pickart, Joan Elliott. *Charade*. Toronto: Bantam Books, Dec. 1984.
————. *Wild Poppies*. Toronto: Bantam Books, May 1987.
Webb, Peggy. *The Joy Bus*. Toronto: Bantam Books, May 1987.

Second Chance at Love

Bates, Jenny. *Dazzled*. New York: Berkley/Jove, Feb. 1984.
Cole, Marianne. *Shining Promise*. New York: Berkley/Jove, Jan. 1984.
Collins, Susanna. *Breathless Dawn*. New York: Berkley/Jove, Jan. 1983.
Curzon, Lucia. *The Dashing Guardian*. New York: Berkley/Jove, May 1983.
Evans, Clair. *Apollo's Dream*. New York: Berkley/Jove, 1982.
Fairfax, Lynn. *Guarded Moments*. New York: Berkley/Jove, Jan. 1983.
Grant, Jeanne. *Man from Tennessee*. New York: Berkley/Jove, May 1983.
Harris, Melinda. *The Wind's Embrace*. New York: Berkley/Jove, Jan. 1983.
Haskell, Mary. *Crazy in Love*. New York: Berkley/Jove, Feb. 1984.
————. *Song for a Lifetime*. New York: Berkley/Jove, June 1983.
Kingston, Meredith. *Long Unveiled*. New York: Berkley/Jove, June 1983.
Larue, Brandy. *Ecstasy Reclaimed*. New York: Berkley/Jove, Jan. 1983.
Mars, Diana. *Sweet Abandon*. New York: Berkley/Jove, May 1983.
————. *Sweet Surrender*. New York: Berkley/Jove, Jan. 1983.
Tierney, Ariel. *Conquering Embrace*. New York: Berkley/Jove, June 1983.
Valcour, Vanessa. *Play It by Heart*. New York: Berkley/Jove, May 1983.

Silhouette Desires

Baker, Judith. *When Last We Loved*. New York: Silhouette Books, 1982.
James, Stephanie. *Corporate Affair*. New York: Silhouette Books, 1982.
Monet, Nicole. *Love's Silver Web*. New York: Silhouette Books, 1982.

Silhouette Intimate Moments

Allison, Möeth. *Love Everlasting*. New York: Silhouette Books, 1983.
Bird, Beverly. *Emeralds in the Dark*. New York: Silhouette Books, 1983.
Bonds, Parris Afton. *Wind Song*. New York: Silhouette Books, 1983.

Christie, Susanna, *Eden's Temptation*. New York: Silhouette Books, April 1987.

James, Kristin. *Dreams of Evening*. New York: Silhouette Books, 1983.

Richards, Emilie. *Bayou Midnight*. New York: Silhouette Books, April 1987.

Roberts, Nora. *Mind over Matter*. New York: Silhouette Books, April 1987.

Simons, Renee. *Colton's Folly*. New York: Silhouette Books, April 1987.

Trevor, June. *Until the End of Time*. New York: Silhouette Books, 1983.

Silhouette Romances

Adams, Pepper. *In Hot Pursuit*. New York: Silhouette Books, May 1987.

Broadrick, Annette. *Circumstantial Evidence*. New York: Silhouette Books, Nov. 1984.

Browning, Dixie. *Renegade Player*. New York: Silhouette Books, 1982.

Dailey, Janet. *The Hostage Bride*. New York: Silhouette Books, 1981.

————. *Wildcatter's Woman*. New York: Silhouette Books, 1982.

Ferrell, Olivia. *High Rider*. New York: Silhouette Books, May 1987.

Goforth, Ellen. *A New Dawn*. New York: Silhouette Books, 1982.

Gordon, Lucy. *A Pearl Beyond Price*. New York: Silhouette Books, May 1987.

Hampson, Anne. *Stardust*. New York: Silhouette Books, 1982.

Hope, Jacqueline. *Love Captive*. New York: Silhouette Books, 1982.

McCarty, Betsy. *The Golden Rose*. New York: Silhouette Books, Nov. 1984.

Michaels, Fern. *Nightstar*. New York: Silhouette Books, 1982.

Michaels, Kasey. *Maggie's Miscellany*. New York: Silhouette Books, 1984.

Paige, Laurie. *A Tangle of Rainbows*. New York: Silhouette Books, Nov. 1984.

Palmer, Diana. *Passion Flower*. New York: Silhouette Books, Nov. 1984.

Parv, Valerie. *The Leopard Tree*. New York: Silhouette Books, May 1987.

Rainville, Rita. *It Takes a Thief*. New York: Silhouette Books, May 1987.

Roberts, Nora. *Song of the West*. New York: Silhouette Books, 1982.

Trent, Brenda. *Hearts on Fire*. New York: Silhouette Books, May 1987.

Silhouette Special Editions

Converse, Jane. *Heartstorm*. New York: Silhouette Books, 1982.

Drummond, Brenna. *Proud Vintage*. New York: Silhouette Books, 1982.

Stephens, Jeanne. *Pride's Posession*. New York: Silhouette Books, 1982.

To Have and To Hold

Connolly, Vivian. *I Know My Love*. New York: Second Chance at Love, Dec. 1983.

Haskell, Mary. *Hold Fast 'Til Dawn*. New York: Second Chance at Love, Dec. 1983.

James, Robin. *The Testimony*. New York: Second Chance at Love, June 1983.

Randolph, Melanie. *Heart Full of Rainbows*. New York: Second Chance at Love, Dec. 1983.

Rose, Jennifer A. *A Taste of Heaven*. New York: Second Chance at Love, Oct. 1983.

Velvet Glove

Doyle, Barbara. *The Hunted Heart*. New York: Avon Books, Nov. 1984.

Flasschoen, Marie. *Fires At Midnight*. New York: Avon Books, Dec. 1984.

Prewit-Parker, Jolene. *Forbidden Dreams*. New York: Avon Books, Nov. 1984.

Smiley, Virginia. *Tender Betrayal*. New York: Avon Books, Dec. 1984.

Other

Frenier's visit to Toronto, April 1984.

"Important Announcement for B. Dalton Bookseller Customers." B. Dalton Bookseller, July 1987.

Lazare, Brenda R., Manager, Business and Legal Affairs, Harlequin Enterprises Limited, letter to author, Dec. 15, 1987.

Second Chance at Love, guidelines. New York: Publishing Group, Oct. 8, 1982.

16th Harlequin Party. Minneapolis: November 1980.

SECONDARY SOURCES

Agena, Kathleen. "The Return of Enchantment." *The New York Times Magazine*, Nov. 27, 1983: 66+.

Allen, Jane E. "Romance Writing Becoming Nation's Newest Cottage Industry." *Minneapolis Star and Tribune*, June 9, 1985: 2G.

Allen, Martha S. "Obscenity Foes Object to Proposal." *Minneapolis Star and Tribune*, Dec. 16, 1983: 1A+.

Allen, Robert C. *Speaking of Soap Operas*. Chapel Hill: University of North Carolina Press, 1985.

Battered Women: An Effective Response. St. Paul, Minn.: Department of Corrections, Programs and Services for Battered Women, 1979.

Bell, Susan G. *Women: From the Greeks to the French Revolution*. Belmont, Cal.: Wadsworth Publishing, 1973.

Bernard, Jessie. *The Future of Marriage*. New York: Bantam, 1973.

Berkeley, Miriam. "In Short." *New York Times Book Review*, Aug. 16, 1984: 16–17.

Brown, Peter. "Gothic Romance Goes Hollywood, But Is the Public Ready for Purity?" *Minneapolis Tribune*, Mar. 29, 1981: 1GX+.

Browne, Ray B. "Popular Culture: The World Around Us." Jack Nachbar, et al., ed. *The Popular Culture Reader*. Bowling Green, Ohio: Bowling Green University Popular Press, 1978: 15–16.

Brozan, Nadine. "Teenage Pregnancy: The Problem that Hasn't Gone Away." *New York Times*, Dec. 20, 1981; (m)57: 1, 17–19.

Butler, Matilda and William Paisley. *Women and the Mass Media: Sourcebook for Research and Action*. New York: Human Sciences Press, 1980.

Campbell, Joseph. "Our Mythology Has Been 'Wiped Out' by Rapid Change." *U.S. News & World Report*, Apr. 16, 1984: 72.

Campion, Kathleen L. "Intimate Strangers: The Readers, the Writers, and the Experts." *MS*, Fall 1983, 11:98–99.

Cawelti, John G. *Adventure, Mystery, and Romance: Formula Stories as Art and Popular Culture*. Chicago: The University of Chicago Press, 1976.

Chodorow, Nancy. *The Reproduction of Mothering: Psychoanalysis and the Sociology of Gender*. Berkeley: University of California Press, 1978.

Collins, Anne. "The Revolution in Romance Novels." *Macleans: Canada's National Magazine*, May 23, 1983, 96:60+, 65–66.

deBeauvoir, Simone. *The Second Sex*. New York: Alfred A. Knopf, 1952.

Douglas, Ann. "Punishing the Liberated Woman: Soft-Porn Culture." *The New Republic*, Aug. 30, 1980: 25–29.

Dowling, Colette. *The Cinderella Complex: Women's Hidden Fear of Independence*. New York: Pocket Books, 1982.

Ehrenreich, Barbara. *Hearts of Men: American Dreams and the Flight from Commitment*. New York: Anchor Books, 1983.

Epstein, Barbara Leslie. *The Politics of Domesticity: Women, Evangelism, and Temperance in Nineteenth-Century America*. Middletown, Conn.: Wesleyan University Press, 1981.

Falk, Kathryn, ed. *How to Write a Romance and Get It Published: With*

Intimate Advice from the World's Most Popular Romantic Writers. New York: Crown, 1983.

Fallon, Eileen. *Words of Love: A Complete Guide to Romance Fiction.* New York: Garland Publishing, 1984.

Falwell, Jerry. *Listen, America!* New York: Bantam, 1981.

Fiedler, Leslie A. "Towards a Definition of Popular Literature." C. W. E. Bigsby, ed. *Superculture: American Popular Culture and Europe.* Bowling Green, Ohio: Bowling Green University Popular Press, 1975: 28–42.

Firestone, Shulamith. *The Dialectic of Sex: The Case for Feminist Revolution.* New York: William Morrow and Co., 1970.

"First Love and Candlelight." *The New York Times*, Feb. 14, 1982: editorial page.

Fishwick, Marshall. "Pop Theology." *The Journal of Popular Culture*, 1969, 3;2: 267–73.

"For Love of Romance Novels." *Minneapolis Star and Tribune*, Sept. 27, 1983: 1C.

French, Marilyn. *The Women's Room.* New York: Jove, 1980.

Frenier, Mariam Darce. "American Anti-Feminist Women: Comparing the Rhetoric of Opponents of the Equal Rights Amendment with That of Opponents of Women's Suffrage." *Women's Studies International Forum*, 1984, 7;6: 455–65.

———. "Barbara Cartland Romances: Going Against Current Realities." Unpublished paper, 1987.

———. "Men's Attitudes as Reflected in Men's Popular Magazines." Unpublished paper presented to the University of Minnesota, Morris, Social Science Seminar, May 1974.

Friday, Nancy. *My Secret Garden: Women's Sexual Fantasies.* New York: Pocket Books, 1973.

Friedan, Betty. *The Feminine Mystique.* New York: Dell, 1963.

Gans, Herbert J. *Popular Culture and High Culture: An Analysis and Evaluation of Taste.* New York: Basic Books, Inc., Harper, 1974.

Gilbert, Sandra M. "Feisty Femme, 40, Seeks Nurturant Paragon." *The New York Times Book Review*, Dec. 30, 1984: 11.

Ginsburg, Faye. "The Body Politic: The Defense of Sexual Restriction by Anti-Abortion Activists." Carole S. Vance, ed. *Pleasure and Danger: Exploring Female Sexuality.* Boston: Routledge & Kegan Paul, 1984: 173–88.

"Harlequin Launches Million-Dollar TV Campaign in US Market." *Publishers Weekly*, Sept. 29, 1975: 38–40.

"Harlequin Operating Profit Down 55%." *Publishers Weekly*, May 25, 1984: 29.

"In Short." *New York Times Book Review*. Aug. 26, 1984: 16.

Jameson, Frederic. "Ideology, Narrative Analysis and Popular Culture." *Theory and Society*, Winter 1977, 4: 543–59.

Jennings, Vivien Lee. "The Romance Wars." *Publishers Weekly*, August 24, 1984: 50–55.

Jensen, Margaret Ann. *Loves $weet Return: The Harlequin Story*. Toronto: Women's Educational Press, 1984.

Kahleck, Melanie. "The Changes in Anne Mather." Unpublished paper presented to the University of Minnesota, Morris, Social Science Seminar, Spring, 1980.

Kellogg, M. A. "The Romance Book Boom." *Seventeen*, May 1983, 42: 158+.

Kolaczyk, Anne. "Romance—From the Reviewer's Side of the Fence." *Romance Writers' Report*, Feb. 1987, 7;1: 42–44.

Kreizenbeck, Alan. "Soaps: Promiscuity and 'New Improved Cheer.'" *The Journal of Popular Culture*, Fall 1983, 17;2: 175–81.

Lake, Randall A. "The Metaethical Framework of Anti-Abortion Rhetoric." *Signs: Journal of Women in Culture and Society*, Spring 1986, 11;3: 478–99.

Lewis, George H. "Between Consciousness and Existence: Popular Culture and the Sociological Imagination." *The Journal of Popular Culture*, Spring 1982, 15;4: 81–92.

Lowery, Marilyn M. *How to Write Romance Novels That Sell*. New York: Rawson Associates, 1983.

Luker, Kristin. *Abortion and the Politics of Motherhood*. Berkeley: University of California Press, 1984.

Martin, Del. *Battered Wives*. New York: Volcano Press, rev. ed., 1981.

Maryles, Daisy. "Harlequin to Launch Mystique Books Via Tested Market Strategies." *Publishers Weekly*, Aug. 28, 1978: 375–76.

——— and Allene Symons. "Love Springs Eternal: Six New Sensual Romance Lines Coming in '83." *Publishers Weekly*, Jan. 14, 1983: 53–56+.

"Mass Market Paperbacks." *Publishers Weekly*, Mar. 13, 1987, 231;8: 27–28.

May, Elaine Tyler. *Great Expectations: Marriage and Divorce in Post-Victorian America*. Chicago: University of Chicago Press, 1980.

May, Lary. *Screening Out the Past: The Birth of Mass Culture and the Motion Picture Industry*. New York: Oxford University Press, 1980.

McDowell, Edwin. "About Books and Authors." *The New York Times Book Review*, March 6, 1983: 38.

———. "The Paperback Evolution." *The New York Times Book Review*, Jan. 10, 1982: 38.

Modleski, Tania. *Loving with a Vengeance: Mass-Produced Fantasies for Women.* Hamden, Conn.: Archon Books, 1982.

Mussel, Kay. *Fantasy and Reconciliation: Contemporary Formulas of Women's Romance Fiction.* Westport, Conn.: Greenwood Press, 1984.

———. "Novels by Subscription: The Harlequin Romance." Unpublished paper delivered at the Tenth Annual Convention of The Popular Culture Association, March 1980.

O'Toole, Patricia. "Paperback Virgins." *Human Behavior*, Feb. 1979: 62–67.

The Pearl: A Journal of Facetiae and Voluptuous Reading. New York: Grove Press, 1968.

Pearson, Carol and Katherine Pope. *The Female Hero in American and British Literature.* New York: R. R. Bowker Company, 1981.

Peele, Stanton with Archie Brodsky. *Love and Addiction.* New York: Taplinger Publishing Company, 1975.

Radway, Janice A. *Reading the Romance: Women, Patriarchy, and Popular Literature.* Chapel Hill: University of North Carolina Press, 1984.

———. "Women Read the Romance: The Interaction of Text and Context." *Feminist Studies*, Spring 1983, 9;1: 53–78.

Reed, J. D. "From Bedroom to Boardroom." *Time*, Apr. 13, 1981: 117: 101+.

Reuter, Madalynne. "S & S to Distribute Harlequin." *Publishers Weekly*, August 24, 1984: 16.

Romantic Times: For Readers of Romantic Fiction. Brooklyn Heights: New York, Romantic Times, Inc., July/August 1981.

Rudolph, Barbara. "Heartbreak Comes to Harlequin." *Forbes*, Mar. 29, 1982, 129: 50–51.

Russ, Joanna. "Somebody's Trying to Kill Me and I Think It's My Husband: The Modern Gothic." Jack Nachbar, et al., ed. *The Popular Culture Reader*, 1978: 280–302.

Schaef, Anne Wilson. *Co-Dependence: Misunderstood-Mistreated.* Minneapolis: Winston Press, 1986.

Shanor, Karen. *The Fantasy Files: A Study of the Sexual Fantasies of Contemporary Women.* New York: Dell, 1977.

Showalter, Elaine. *A Literature of Their Own: British Women Novelists from Brontë to Lessing.* Princeton: Princeton University Press, 1977.

Smith, Don. "The Social Content of Pornography." *Journal of Communication*, 1976, 26: 16–24; cited in Butler and Paisley. *Women and the Mass Media*, 1980.

Smith, Dwayne and Marc Matre. "Social Norms and Sex Roles in Romance and Adventure Magazines." *Journalism Quarterly*, 1975, 52: 309–15; cited in Butler and Paisley. *Women and the Mass Media*, 1980.

Snitow, Ann Barr. "Mass Market Romance: Pornography for Women is Different." *Radical History Review*, Spr/Sum 1979, 20: 140–61.

Stickler, Jeff. "Perpetual Over-Sleeper Wakes Up to Career as Author." *Minneapolis Tribune*, Oct. 23, 1981: 6C.

Sullerot, Evelyne. *Women On Love: Eight Centuries of Feminine Writing*. New York: Doubleday, 1979.

Tannahill, Reah. *Sex in History*. New York: Stein & Day, 1980.

Tavris, Carol and Carole Offir. *The Longest War: Sex Differences in Perspective*. New York: Harcourt Brace Jovanovich, 1977.

Thirty Years of Harlequin, 1949–1979. Toronto: Harlequin Books, 1979.

Thurston, Carol. "The Liberation of Pulp Romances." *Psychology Today*, April 1983, 17: 14–15.

———. "Popular Historical Romances: Agent for Social Change? An Exploration of Methodologies." *The Journal of Popular Culture*, Summer 1985, 19;1: 35–49.

———. "Romance Readers—A 'Moving Target.' " *Romance Writers' Report*, Feb. 1987, 7;1: 20–22.

———. "Romance Readers—The Moving Target Moves On (Part 2)." *Romance Writers' Report*, April 1987, 7;2: 12–14.

Thurston, Carol. *The Romance Revolution: Erotic Novels for Women and the Quest for a New Sexual Identity*. Urbana: University of Illinois Press, 1987.

Thurston, Carol and Barbara Doscher. "Supermarket Erotica: Bodice-Busters Put Romantic Myths to Bed." *The Progressive*, Apr. 1982, 46: 49–51.

Truehart, Charles. "Strong Women and Caring Men: New Models Unveiled at 2nd Romance Writers Meeting." *Publishers Weekly*, June 25, 1982: 23–24.

Tuckman, Gaye. "Women's Depiction by the Mass Media." *Signs: Journal of Women in Culture and Society*, Spring 1979, 4;3: 528–42.

Wagner, Susan. "Justice Warns Harlequin on Pinnacle Acquisitions." *Publishers Weekly*, Feb. 26, 1976: 97.

Walters, Ray. "Paperback Talk." *The New York Times Book Review*, Mar. 16, 1980: 35–36.

———. "Paperback Talk." *The New York Times Book Review*, Jan. 17, 1982: 35–36.

———. "Paperback Talk." *The New York Times Book Review*, May 9, 1982: 35–36.

Welleck, Rene and Austin Warren. *Theory of Literature.* London: Jonathan Cape, 1949.

Weitzman, Lenore J. *The Divorce Revolution: The Unexpected Social and Economic Consequences for Women and Children in America.* New York: The Free Press, 1985.

Wood, Leonard, ed. "The Gallup Survey: The Books Women Buy." *Publishers Weekly,* May 22, 1987, 231;20: 27.

Wood, Leonard A. "Romance, Biography Top Lists of Books Women Buy." *Publishers Weekly,* Dec. 2, 1983: 30.

Woodruff, Juliette. "A Spate of Words, Full of Sound and Fury, Signifying Nothing: Or, How to Read in Harlequin." *The Journal of Popular Culture,* Fall 1985, 19;2: 25–32.

Wright, Will. *Sixguns & Society: A Structural Study of the Western.* Berkeley: University of California Press, 1975.

Yankelovich, Skelly and White. *Consumer Research Study on Reading and Book Publishing.* London: The Book Industry Study Group, 1978.

————. *The 1978 Consumer Research Study on Reading and Bookbuying Habits of the American Public.* n.p.: The Book Industry Study Group, 1978.

Index

About the Author

MARIAM DARCE FRENIER, Associate Professor of History at the University of Minnesota, Morris, has published articles and chapters on American romance fiction, American anti-feminist attitudes, the role of women in the People's Republic of China, and other subjects related to women's studies.